THE ENGLISH ANGEL

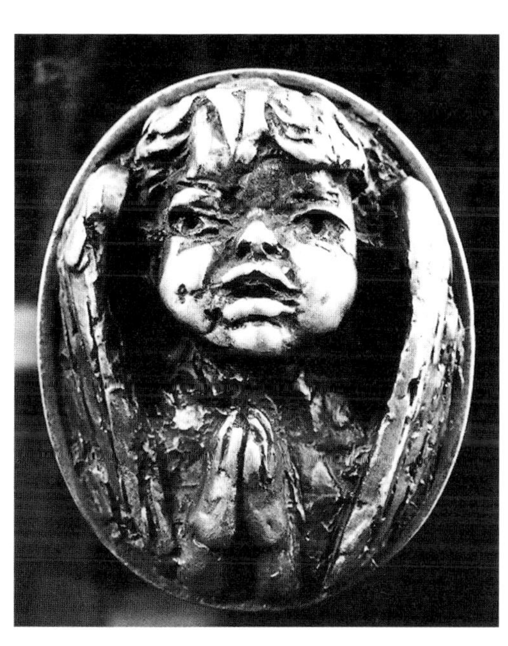

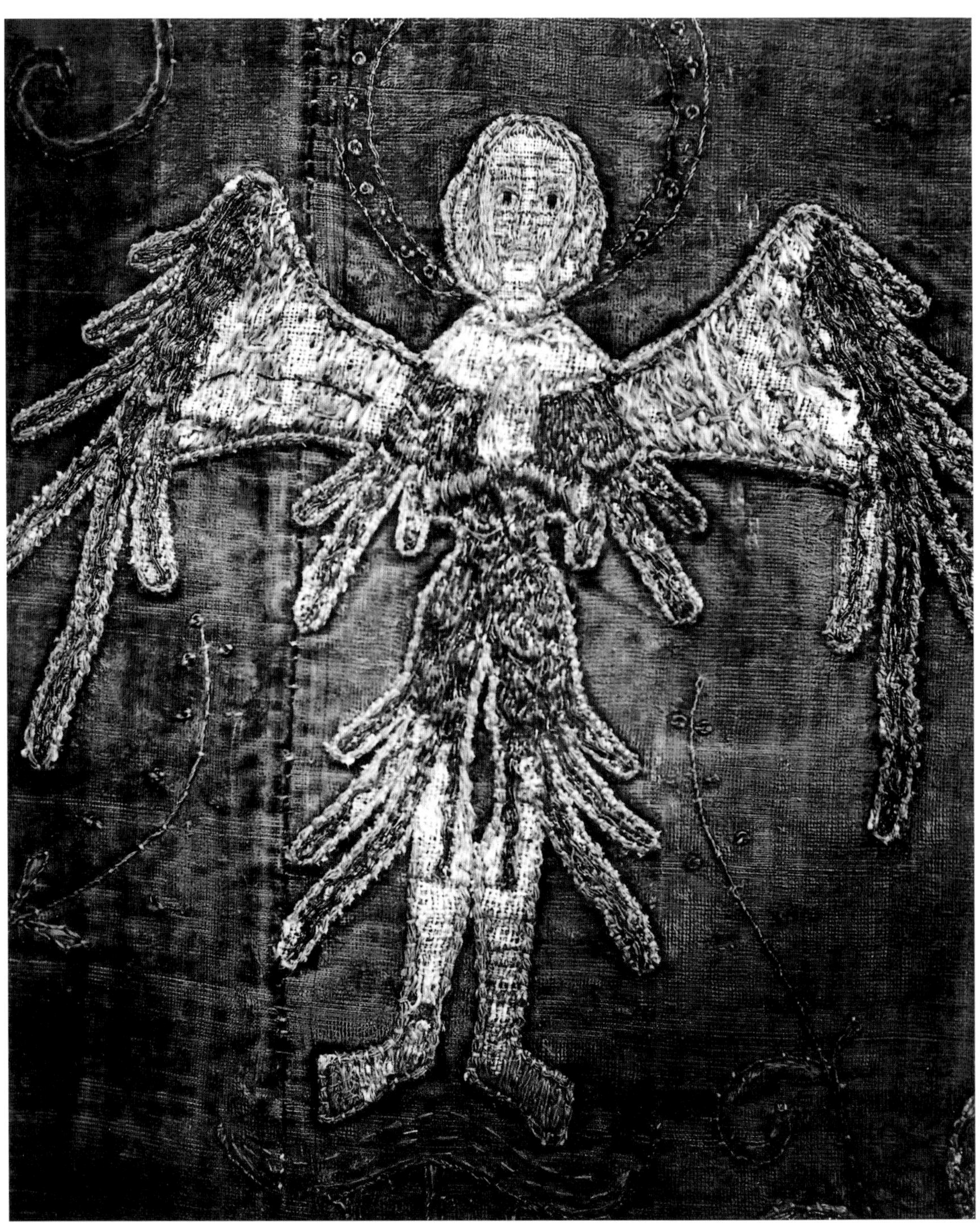

To Liz and Hester

THE ENGLISH ANGEL

PETER BURTON &

HARLAND WALSHAW

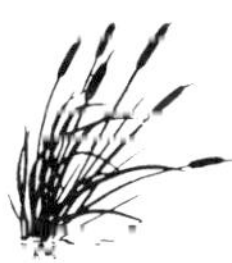

THE WINDRUSH PRESS · GLOUCESTERSHIRE

First published in Great Britain by
The Windrush Press in 2000
Little Window, High Street
Moreton-in-Marsh
Gloucestershire GL56 0LL
Tel: 01608 652012
Fax: 01608 652125
Email: Windrush@windrushpress.com
Website: www.windrushpress.com

Text and photographs Copyright © Peter Burton and Harland Walshaw 2000

The right of Peter Burton and Harland Walshaw to be identified as copyright holders of this work has been asserted by them in accordance with the Copyright, Designs and Patents Act 1988

British Library in Cataloguing Data
A catalogue record for this book is available from the British Library

ISBN 1 900624 43 5
Cover design Miranda Harvey
Typeset by Mark-making Design Ltd
Printed and bound in Slovenia
by Printing House Mladinska knjiga, Ljubljana
by arrangement with Korotan, Ljubljana

The photograph on page 1 is of a bronze doorknob in the form of a cherub by Jacob Epstein, on the main entrance doors to Coventry Cathedral.
Page 3 shows a detail of the Culmstock Cope, a 14th century textile displayed in Culmstock church, and probably embroidered only a few miles away in the Devon village of Prescott. A fine example of opus anglicanum *on a velvet background.*

To order your free Windrush Press catalogue featuring general history,
travel books and other titles, please phone us on
01608 652012 or **01608 652025**
Fax us on **01608 652125** Email: **Windrush@windrushpress.com**
Website: **www.windrushpress.com**
Or write to:
The Windrush Press Limited
Little Window, High Street, Moreton-in-Marsh
Gloucestershire, GL56 0LL, UK

Angles & Angels

The Venerable Bede tells the story of the slave boys from Northumbria in the Forum at Rome. St Gregory, struck by their fair hair and blue eyes, asks their nationality. When told that they are Angles, he replies, with one of those rare puns that work in two languages, *'Non Angli, sed angeli.'* Not Angles, but angels.

Even so, we would not consider ourselves to be the most angelic of nations. Yet when you begin to look closely at our buildings and our monuments, our pubs and our cemeteries, our churches, lamp posts and theatres, you realise that we are a country infested by angels, in almost plague-like proportion: lurking in the hammer-beams, squatting on the gravestones, cherubim and seraphim floating in the vaulting. On ships' prows and shop fronts, on inn signs and organ cases, on floor tiles and roof bosses, winged figures decorate our world, haunting this godless age with the image of a spiritual past: heralds of God, their message now unheeded.

The profusion of angel carving, in church architecture, civic monument, and folk art, constitutes a decorative tradition which, if not exclusively English, has no parallel for its range and invention in any other country. There are famous foreign angels, such as those of Giselbertus in Autun, or the smiling angel of Reims; and Italian painting swarms with the creatures. But in England, no cathedral is complete without its celestial host, no graveyard without its guardians of the dead; and Anglo-angels play a secular role that leads them into places where you think they would fear to tread.

Nor are angels confined to the distant past. Some of the most powerful images in this book come from the twentieth century, and the piece of modern sculpture that has caught the public imagination is Anthony Gormley's Angel of the North, its glinting wings embracing the motorway traffic.

Angels have also inhabited the imagination of English writers down the centuries. 'Most men know the make of angels and archangels,' wrote Lord Byron, 'since there's scarce a scribbler has not one to show.' Most twentieth century scribblers, more surprisingly, had an angel to show: from Robert Bridges to Ted Hughes, the poets laureate met their angels and relayed their messages. After all, the beginnings of English literature were angelically inspired. Caedmon, the first English poet, was a herdsman at Whitby Abbey when he was visited by an angel in a dream, who instructed him to write songs in his native tongue. Few poets who followed in his footsteps quite forgot their debt to Caedmon's angel.

England is a country where angel footsteps have often trod. A pilgrimage to angelic sites would take us to the shrine of Our Lady of Walsingham, repositioned by angels on firmer foundations while the builders slept; to Glastonbury Tor, where St Joseph and his community of hermits were guided by the Archangel Gabriel to build the first Christian church in Britain; to St Michael's Mount off the Cornish coast, where in AD 495 some fishermen saw the blessed Archangel on a rocky ledge, and where miraculous cures for the toothache were reported after his divine intercession; and to the tomb of the first English historian, Bede himself, recorder of others' angelic experiences, whose epitaph was completed by an angel while the stone carver paused, searching for a suitable adjective: it was the angel who gave to Bede the posthumous title, 'Venerable'.

The history of angels in England is rich, varied and long, lasting from before the time of Bede, and unfinished yet.

If God is dead, his angels have survived him.

Peter Burton and Harland Walshaw
June 2000

Right: The angels on the glass screen which separates the new Coventry Cathedral from the ruins of the bombed building were engraved by John Hutton.

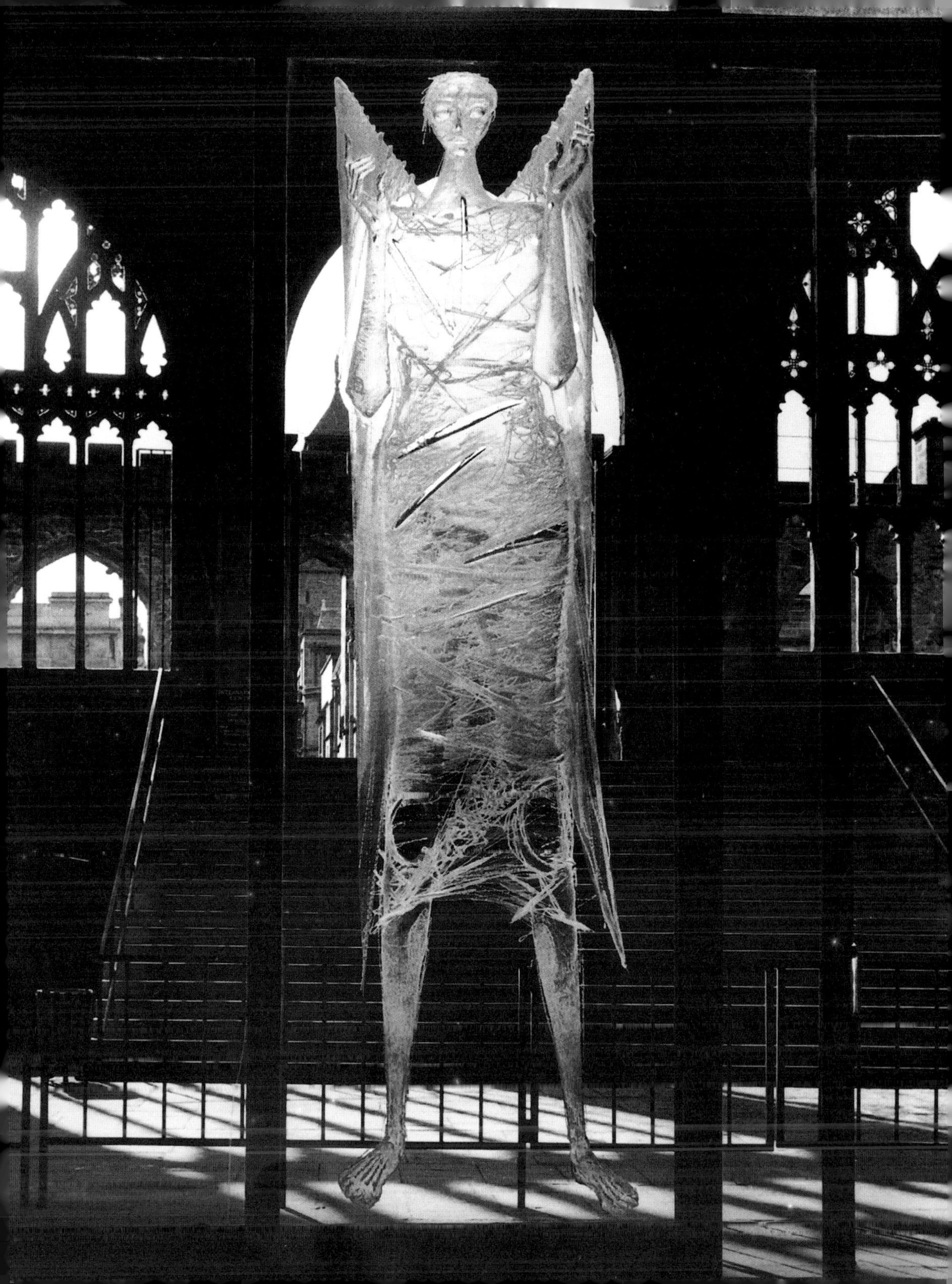

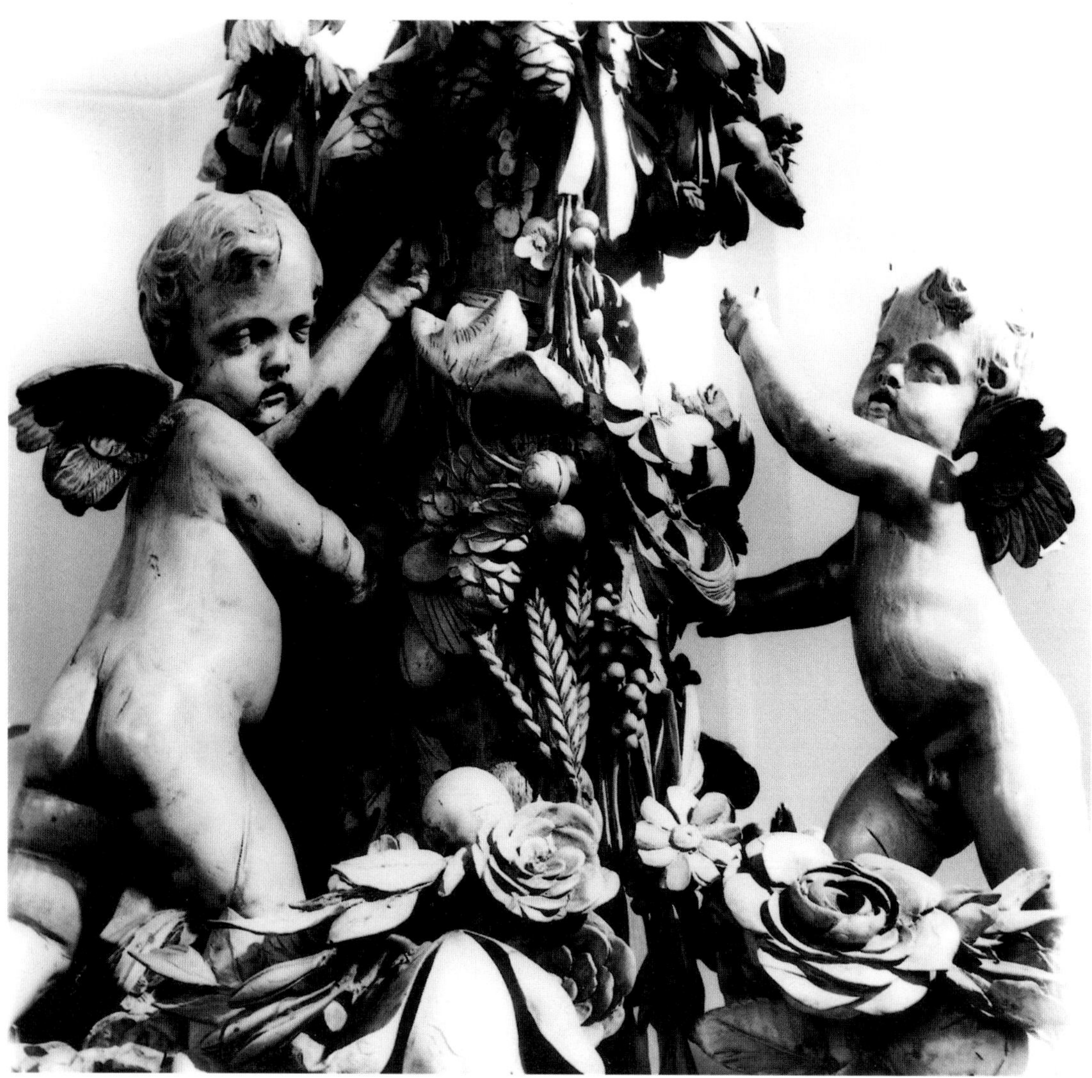

Grinling Gibbons angels, carved in limewood, on the font cover of All Hallows by the Tower.

An angel from the former altar of
Whitehall chapel, now sitting on a
window sill in Burnham-on-Sea.
Carved in 1686 by Grinling Gibbons
or his master Arnold Quellin.

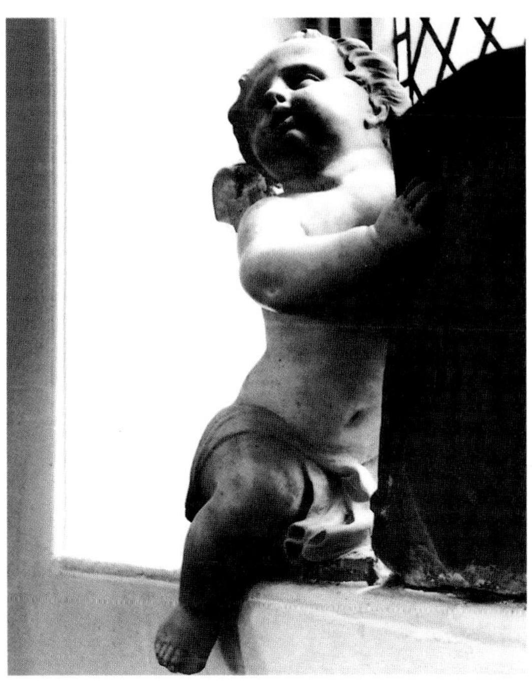

These singing angels,
which are directly
above the entrance to
Mansion House tube
station, are on the
porch of Hawksmoor's
City of London church,
St Mary Woolnoth.

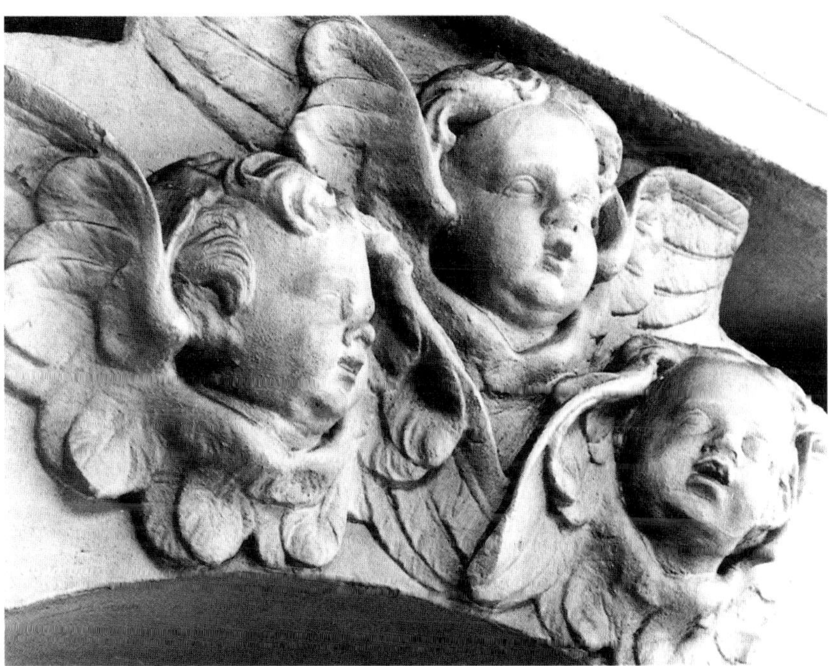

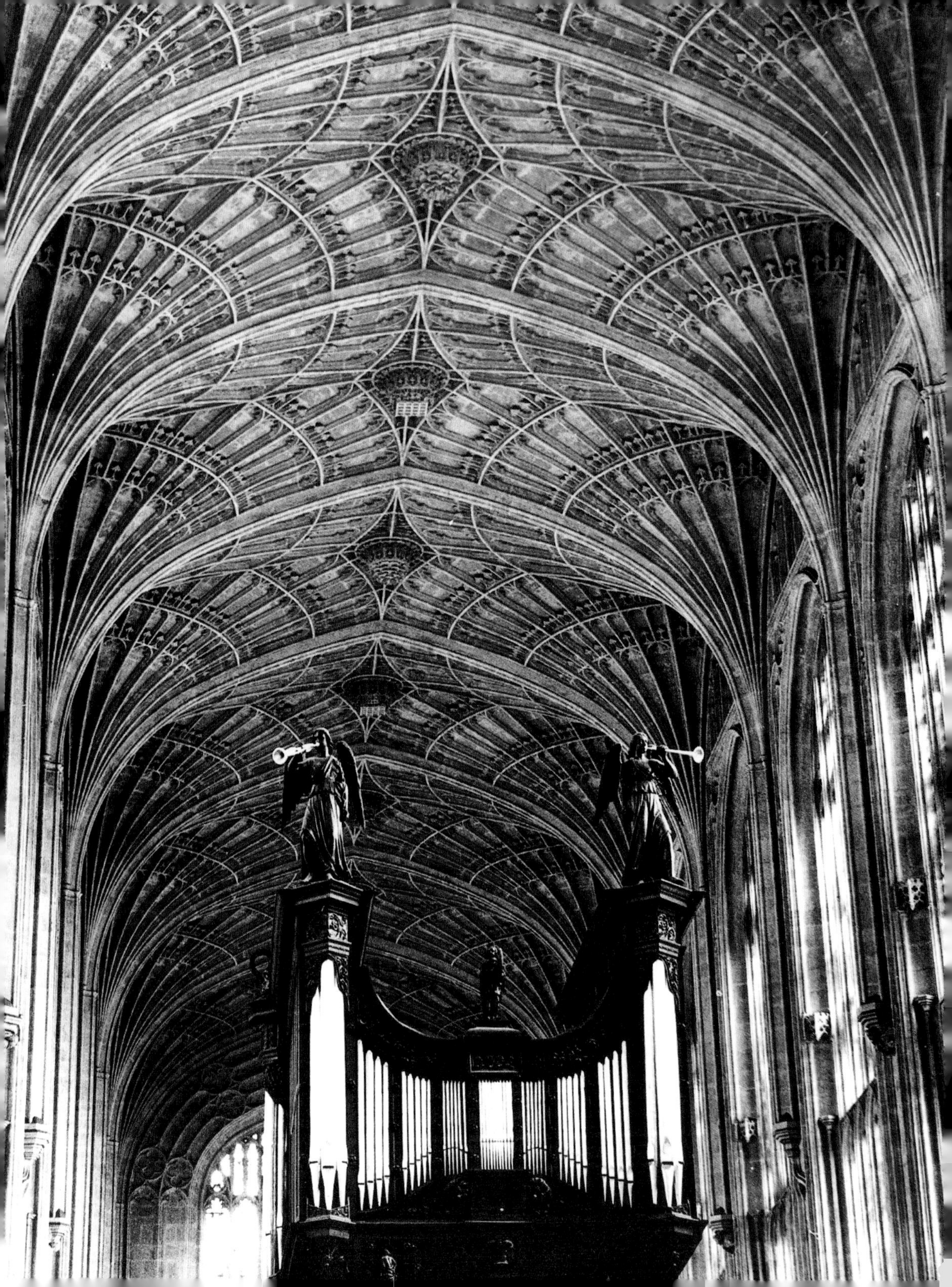

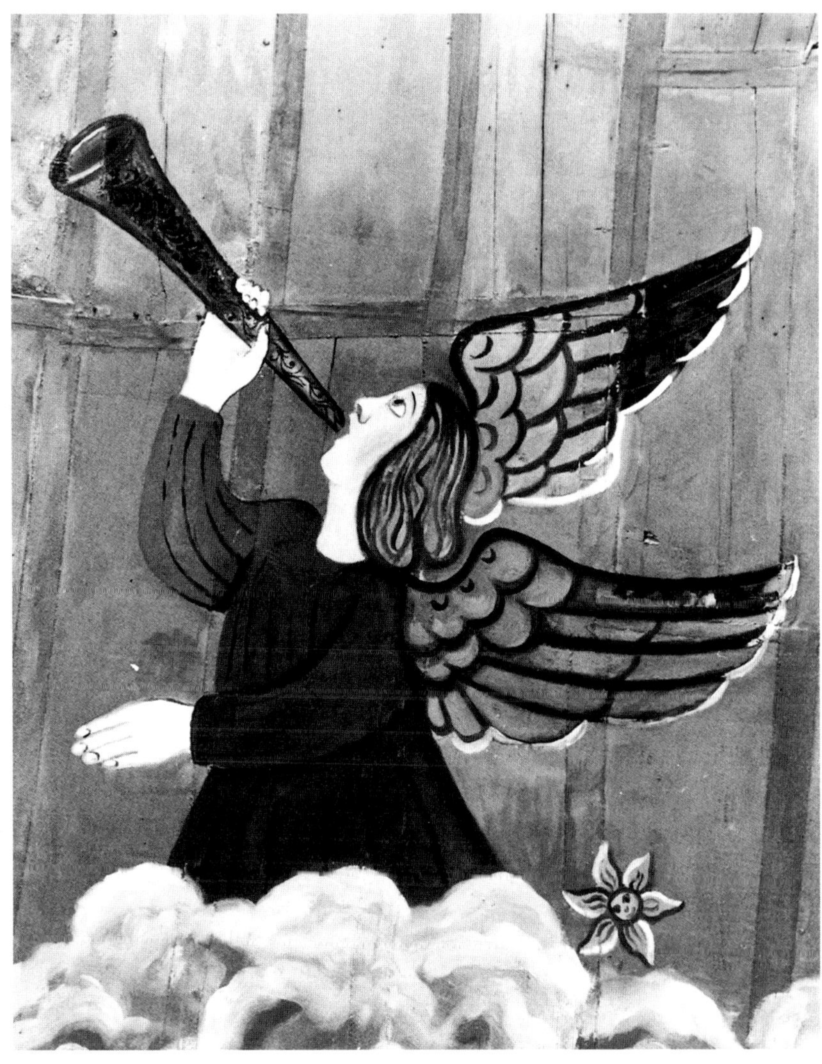

17th century trumpeting angel, painted on wood in Gwydir Uchaf Chapel, Gwynedd.

Left: The fan vaulting of King's College Chapel, Cambridge, shelters a 17th century organ. The angels blowing trumpets are of 1859, and were modelled by Sir George Gilbert Scott on the original figures, which appear in an engraving of 1690.

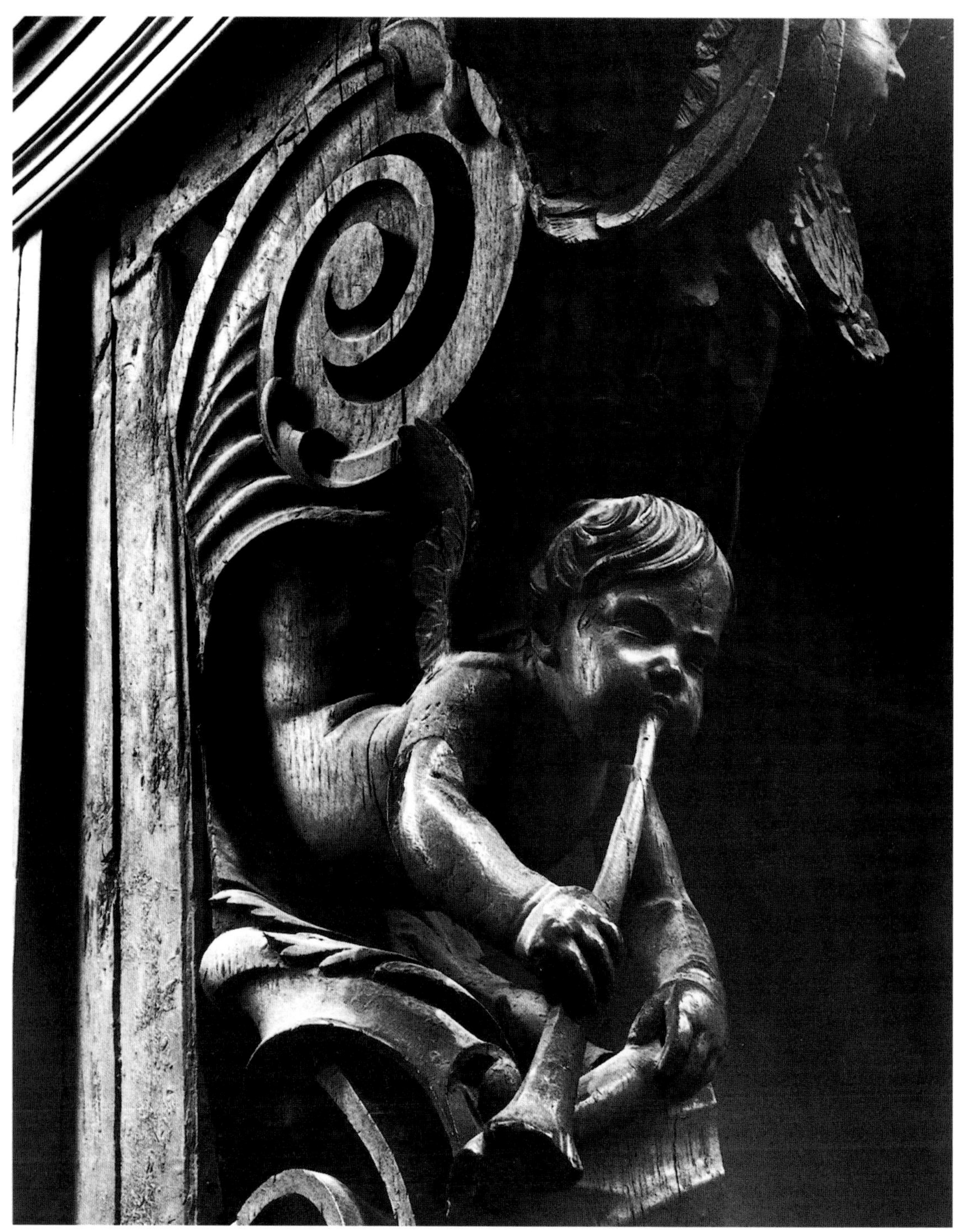

Angel on an organ case, St Helen's, Bishopsgate, City of London.

A visiting angel, English by adoption. This wonderfully carved baroque musician is said to have come from a Dutch ship, but now sits with two companions underneath the pulpit at Trowse Newton near Norwich.

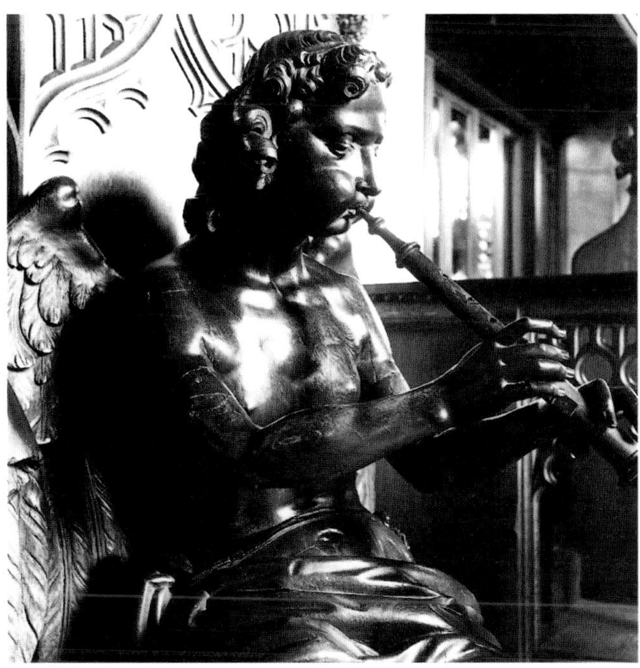

Engraved glass by John Hutton in the south transept of Guildford Cathedral, consecrated in 1961.

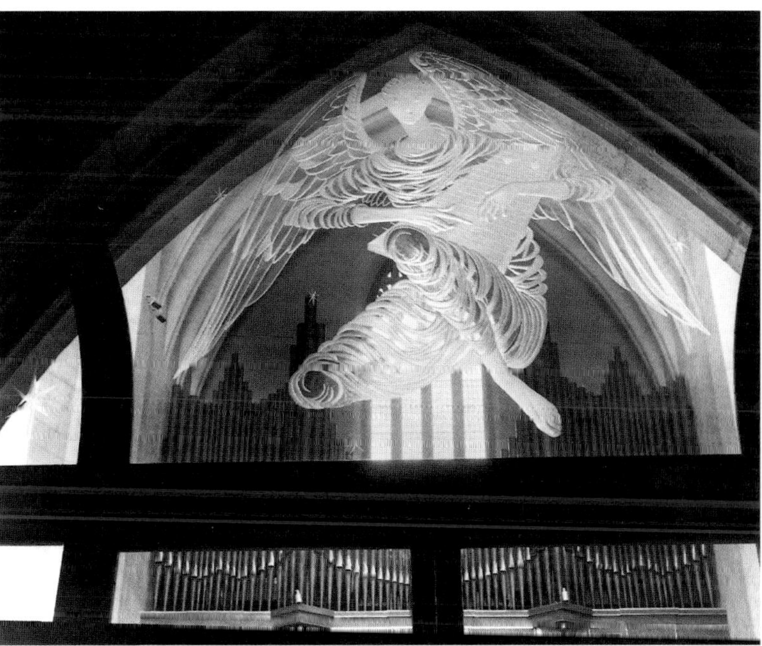

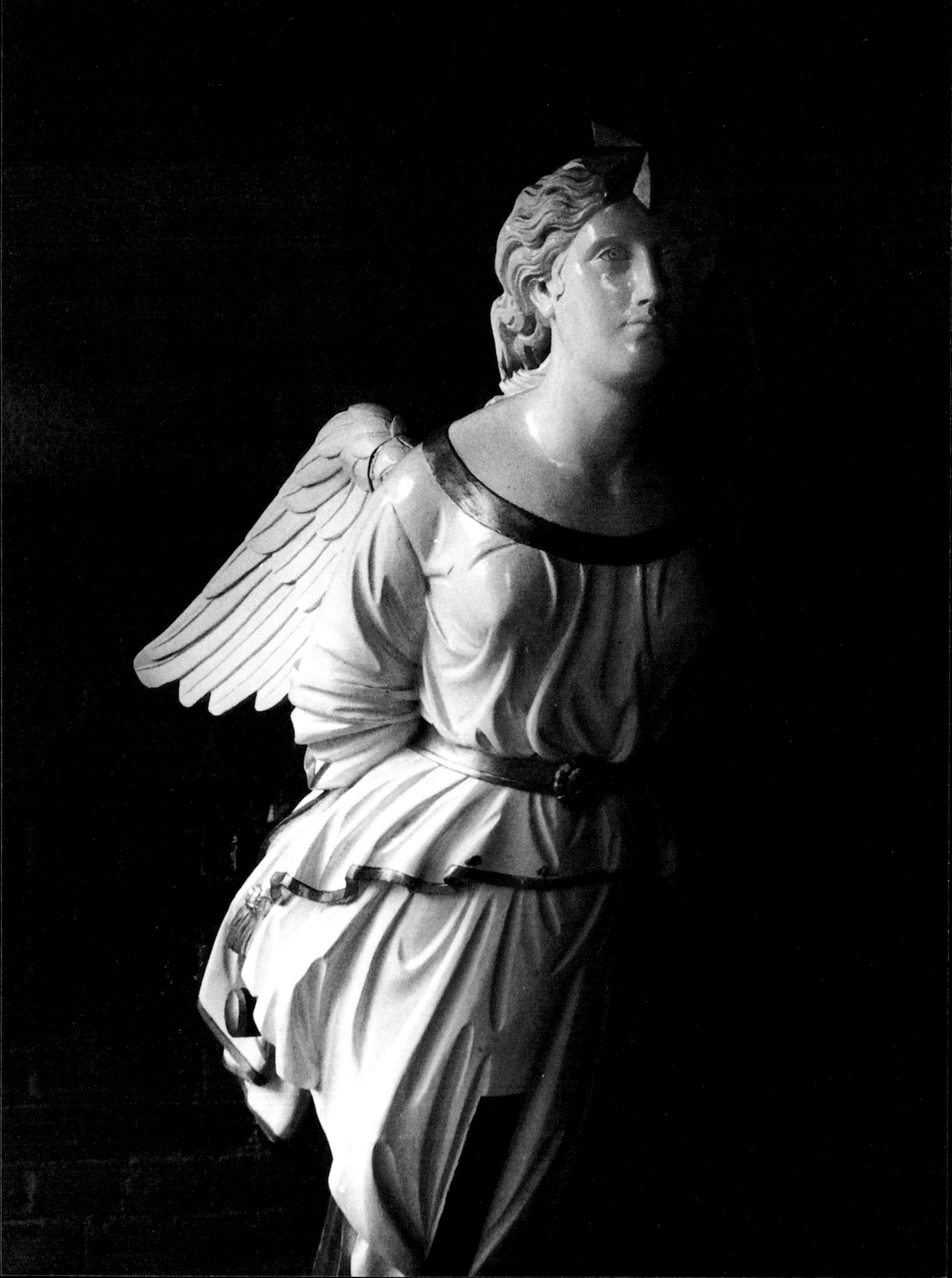

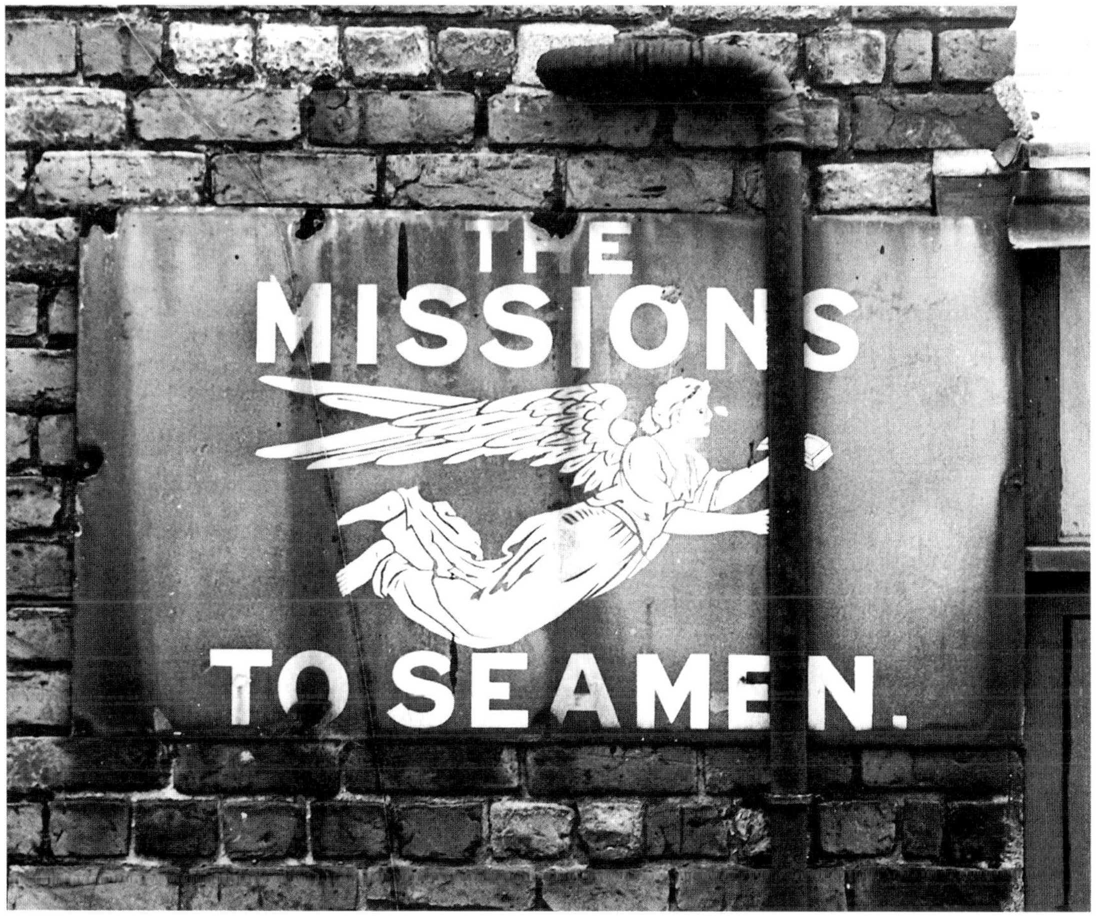

The flying angel was adopted by The Missions to Seamen in 1858, only two years after it was established. There have been four different designs since then, and this 1930s version, photographed in Whitby in the 1950s, was superseded by one commissioned from the artist Eric Fraser, which lasted until the end of the century. With the recent change of name to The Mission to Seafarers, a new logo-like design has seen the angel lose its book (here half-hidden by a drainpipe).

Left: This figurehead was one of a series of 20, carved in Plymouth for an Indian shipping line. It never reached India, for the ship carrying the commission was wrecked off Rame Head. Three of the figureheads were saved, and this angel is now on display in the colonnade ot Antony House in Cornwall.

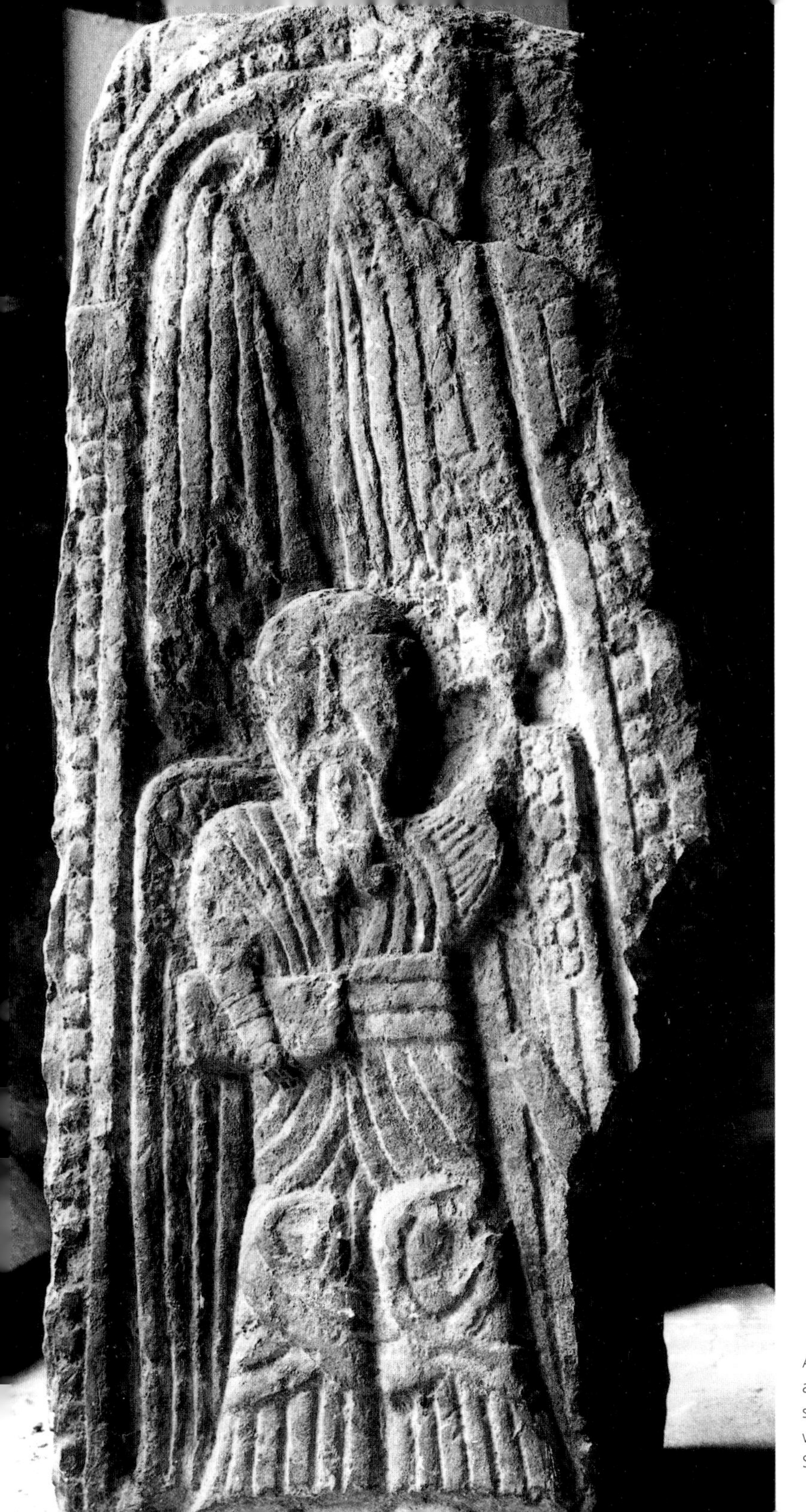

An angel holding a book, on a fragment of Anglo-Saxon stone carving, standing on a window sill in the church at Shelford, near Nottingham.

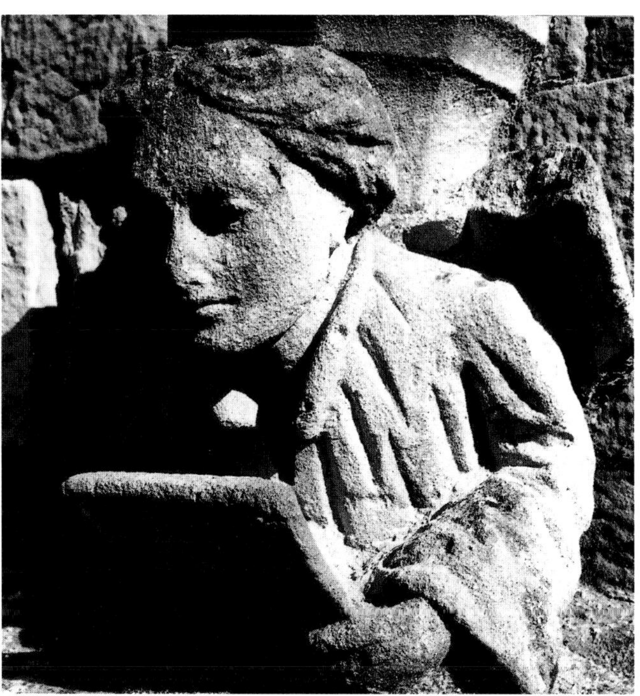

Angel reading on the porch of
Lympstone church, Devon.

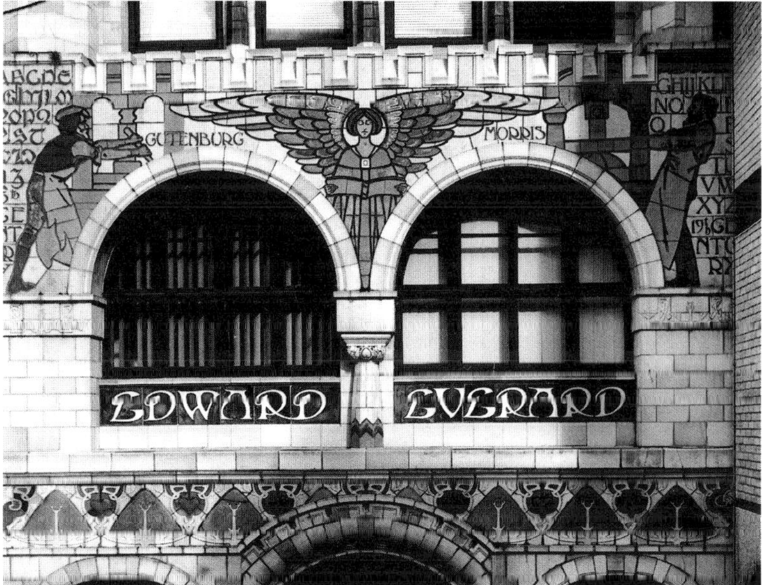

Edward Everard was a Bristol
printer, and the Art Nouveau
façade, which pays homage
to Gutenberg and William
Morris, was designed in
1900 by Henry Williams.

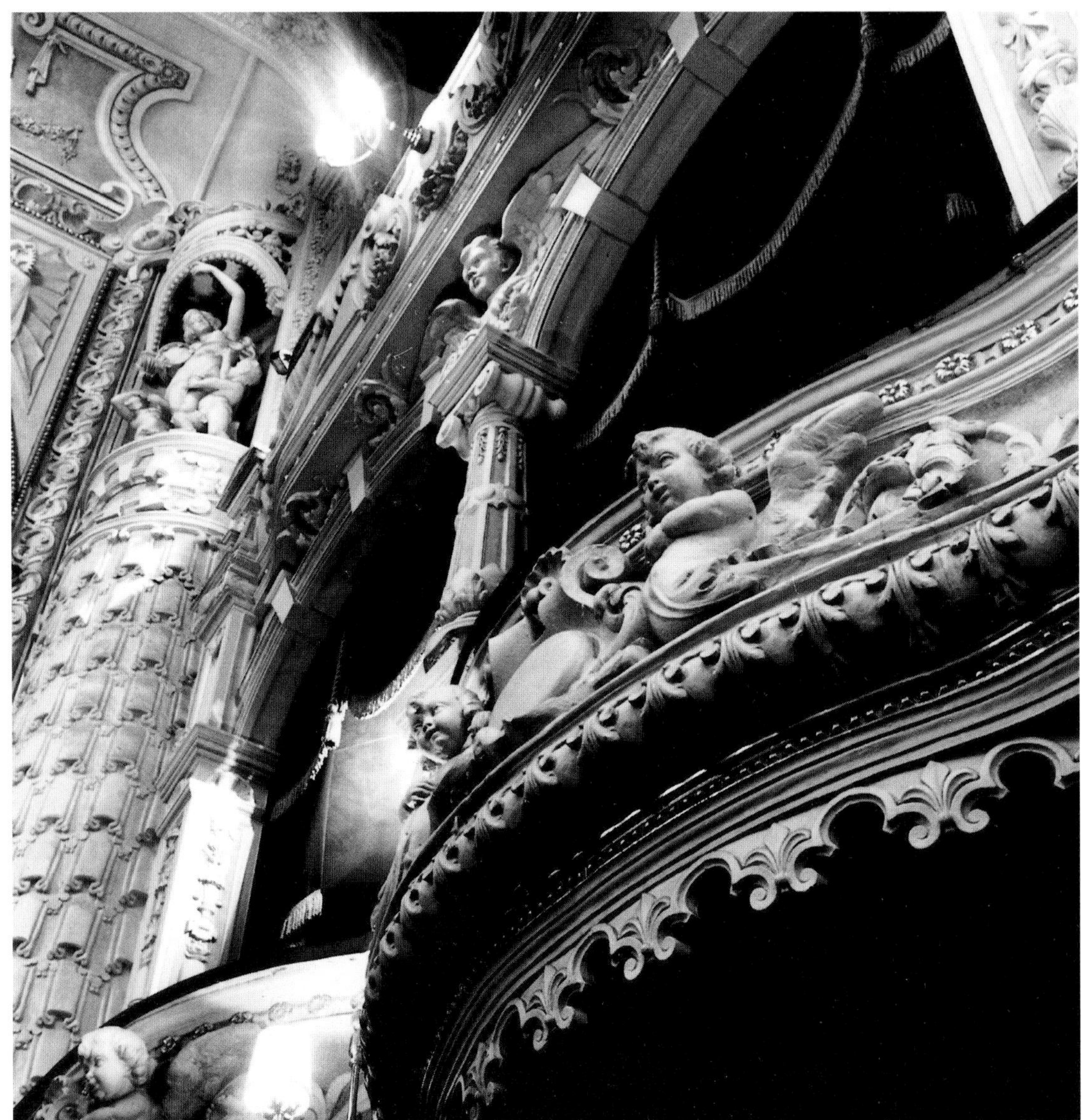

Theatrical angels adorn the theatre at Richmond-on-Thames,
by the great Victorian theatre architect, Frank Matcham.

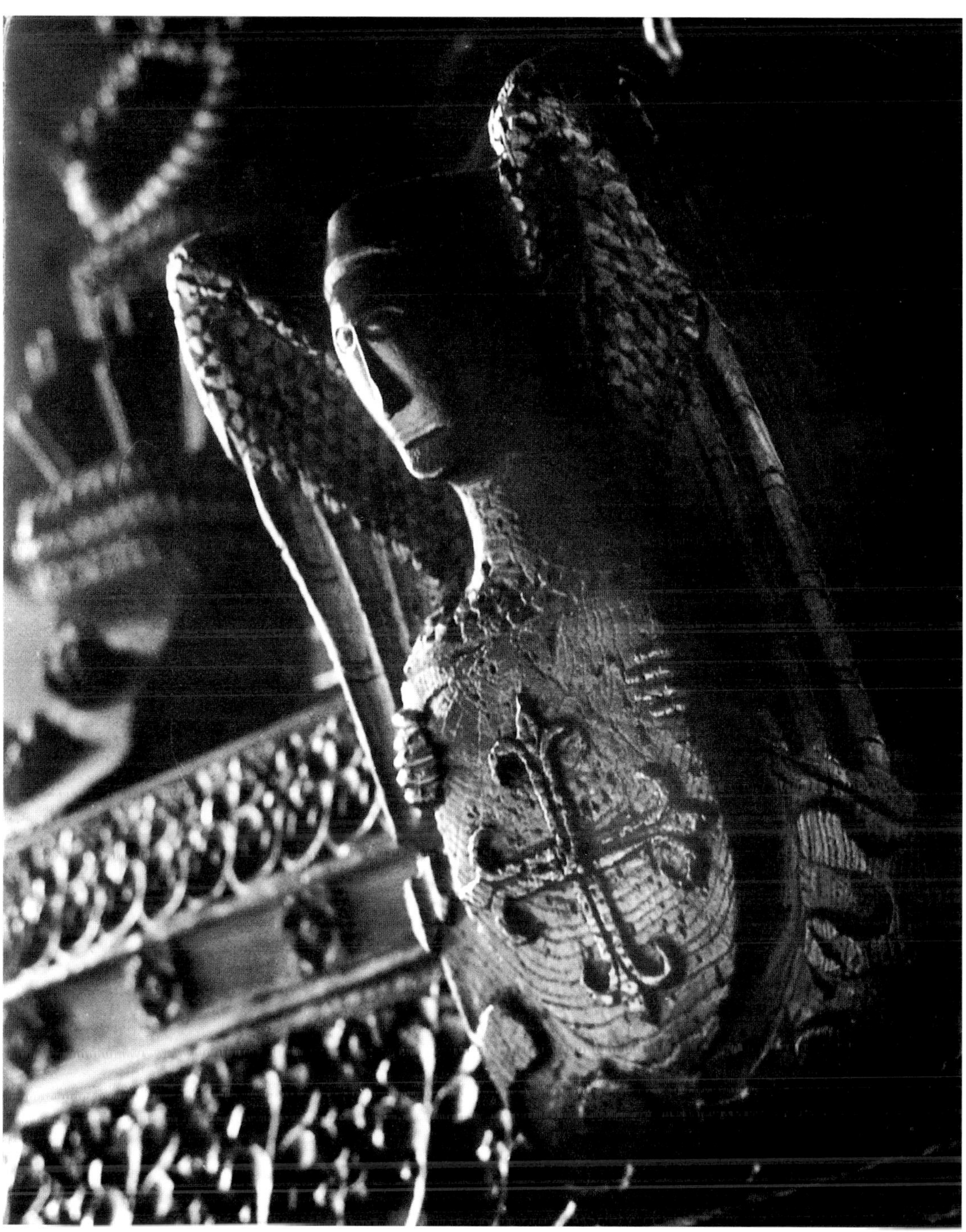

This angel, on the moveable mediaeval screen in Rufford Old Hall, may have observed performances by the young Shakespeare, who is rumoured to have been a member of an acting troupe in this Lancashire house, home of the Heskeths.

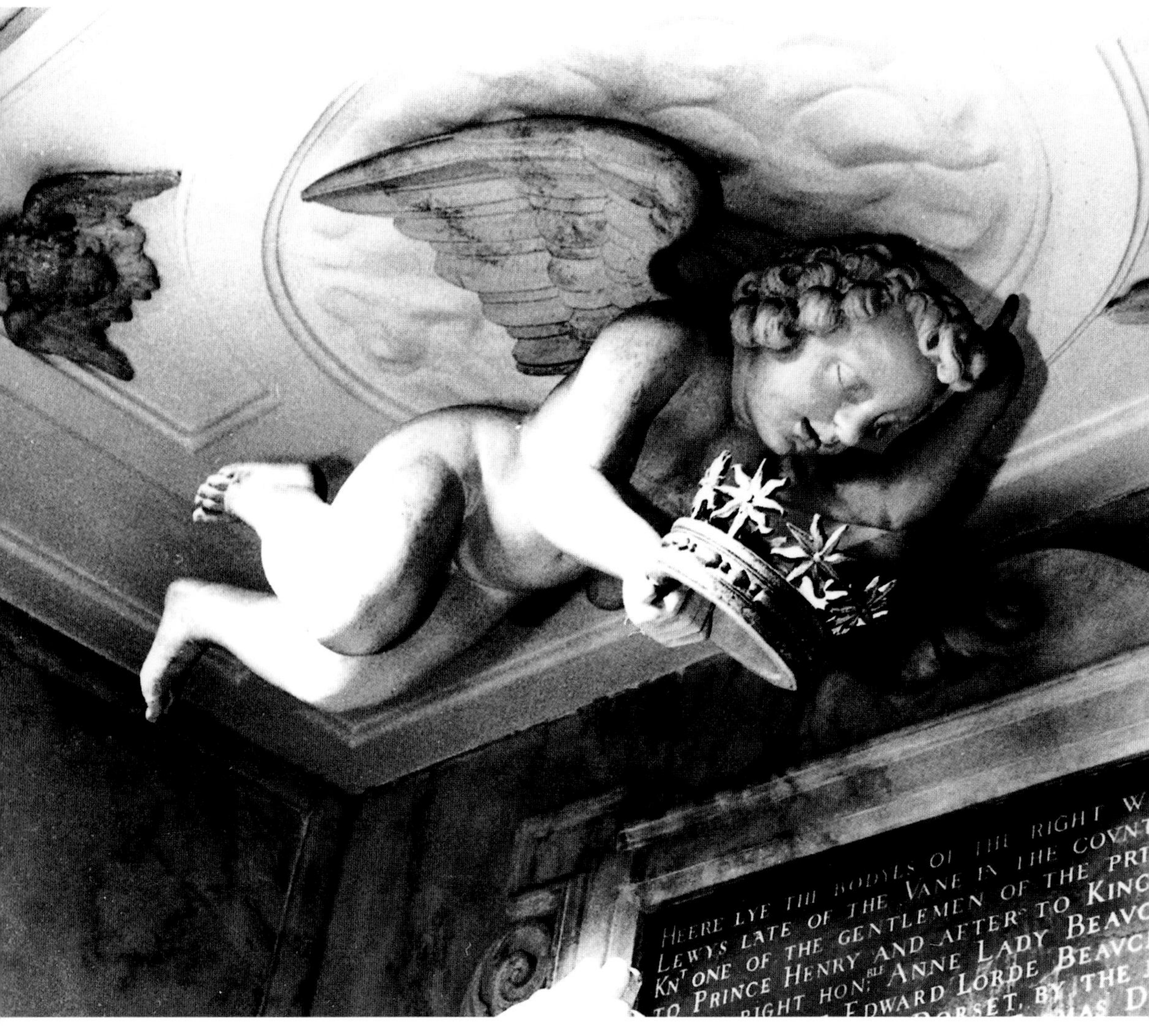

The crown-bearing angel flies over the tomb of Sir Edward Lewys (died 1630)
and his wife, Lady Anne Beauchamp, at Edington Priory in Wiltshire.

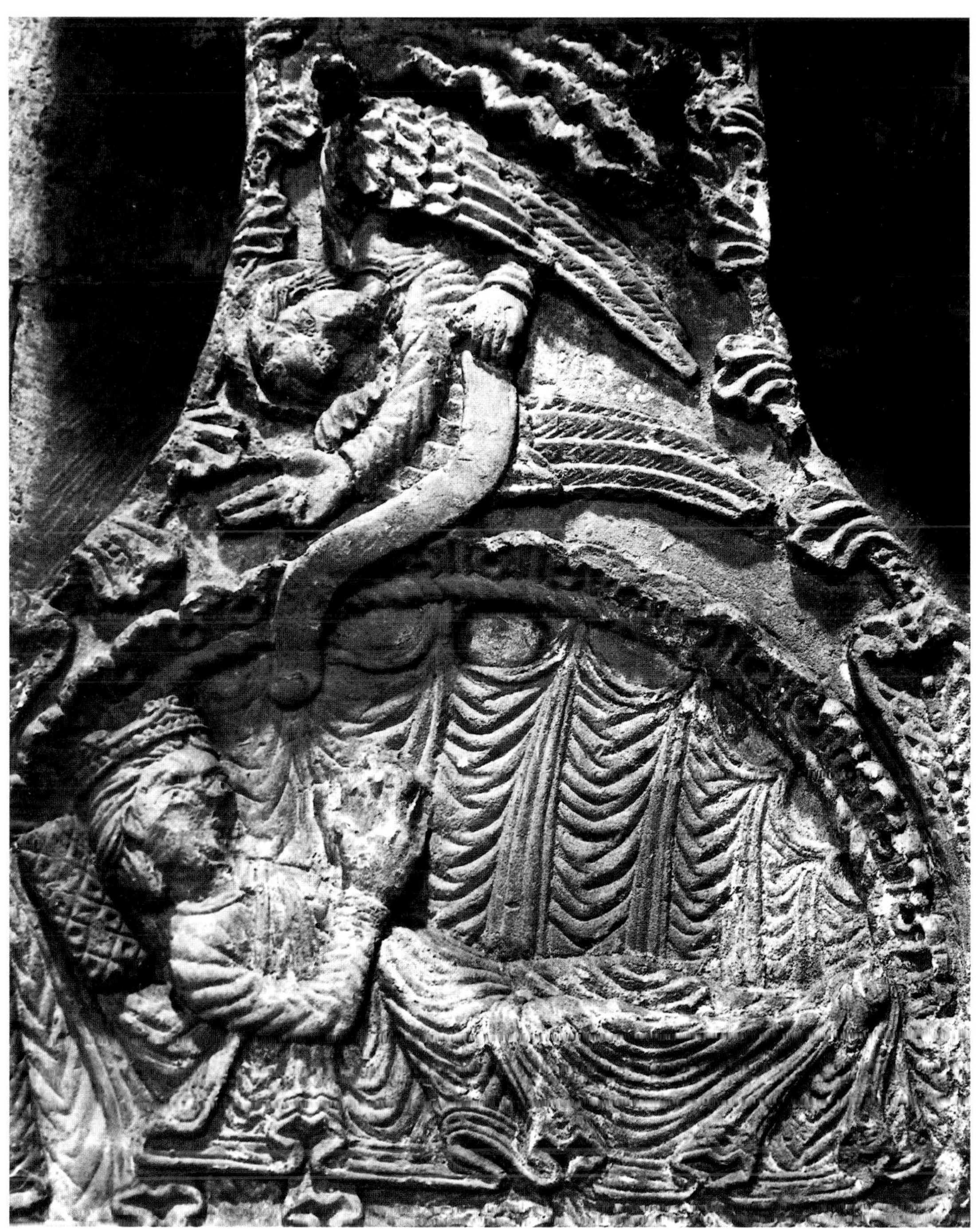

An angel appears to the Empress Helena in a dream, to tell her where to find the True Cross, in this Norman carving on a cross at Church Kelloe, County Durham.

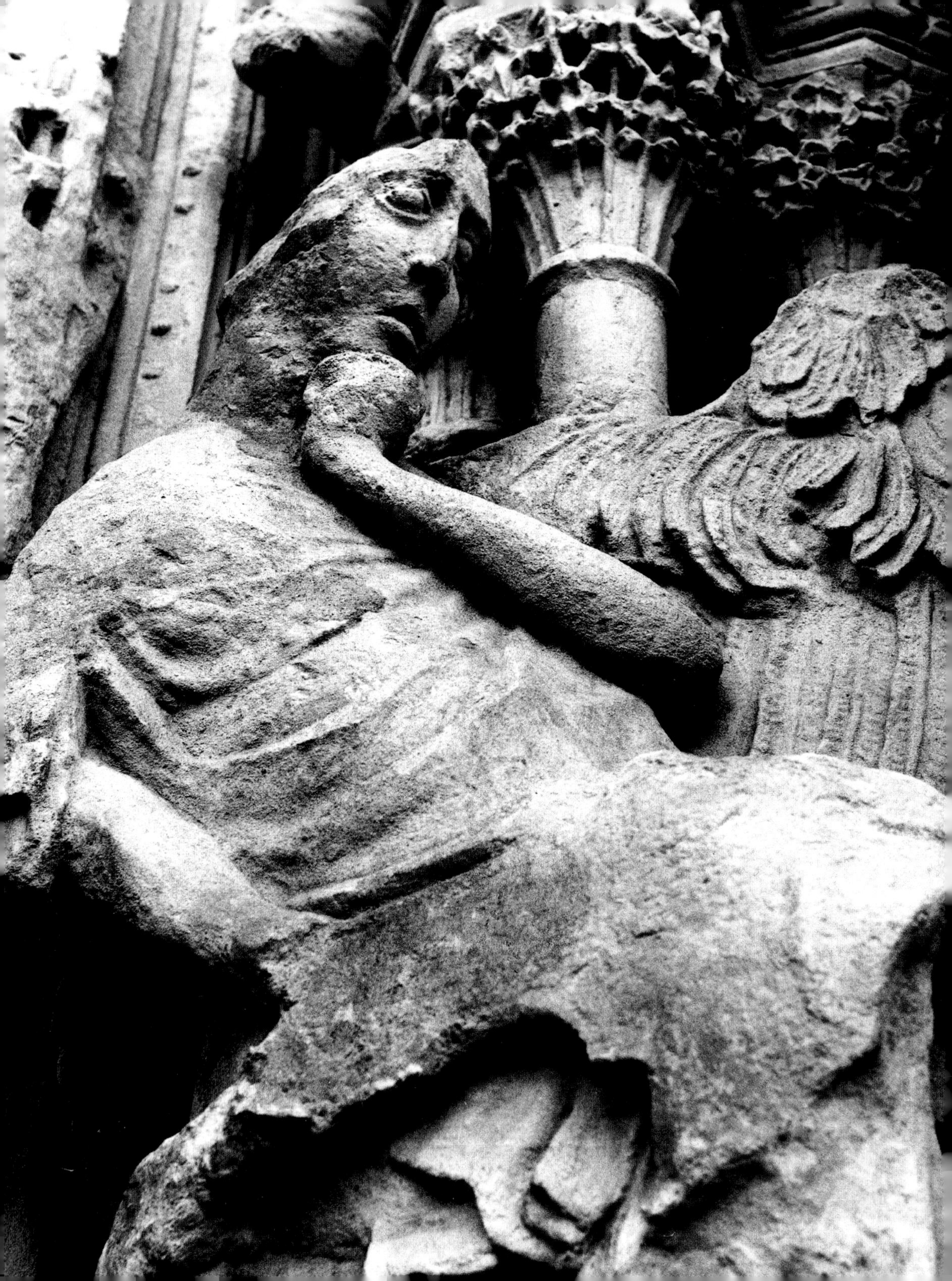

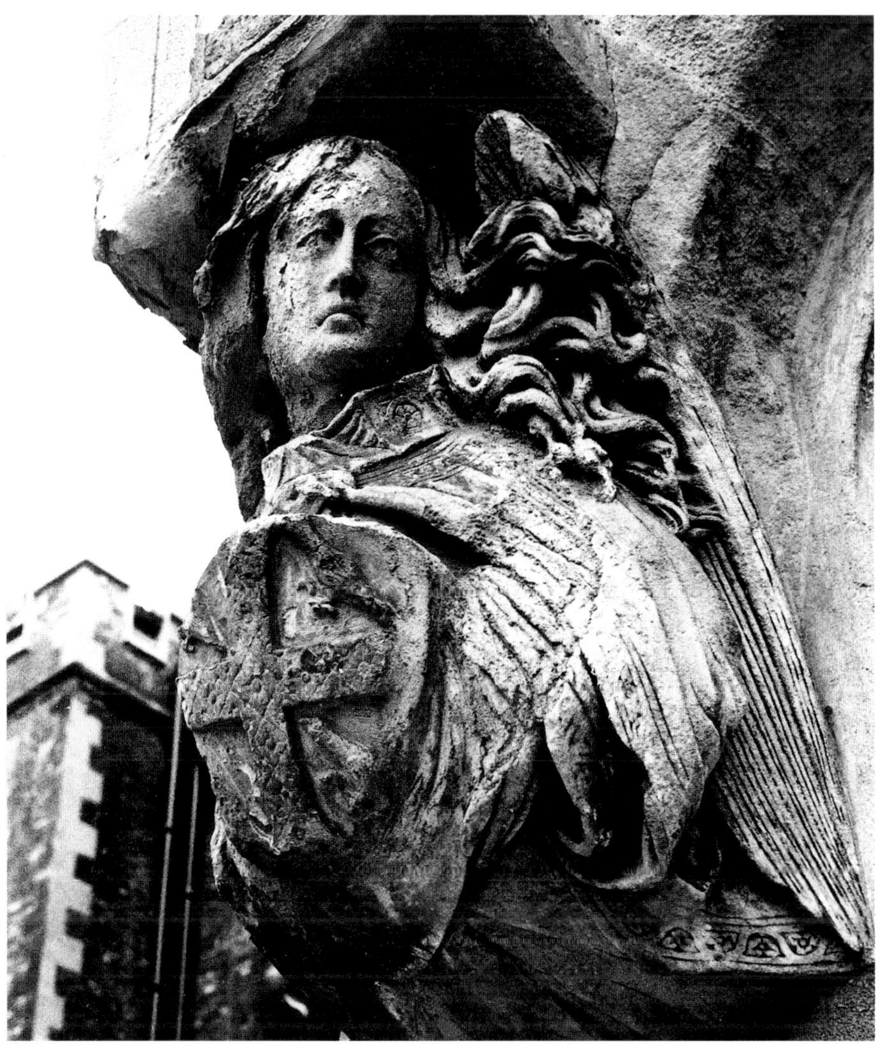

Shield-bearing angel by a doorway in Dean's Yard, Westminster School.

Left: The screen on the west front of Exeter Cathedral was carved from local Beer stone in about 1350. There are three tiers of figures: Apostles on top, Kings of Judah in the middle, and the bottom one entirely angels. It is the angels who have suffered most damage from weathering, pollution and the vandalism of Cromwellian iconoclasts. Most have lost their heads, one or two have been replaced or restored, but a few worn faces remain, to gaze enigmatically across the centuries.

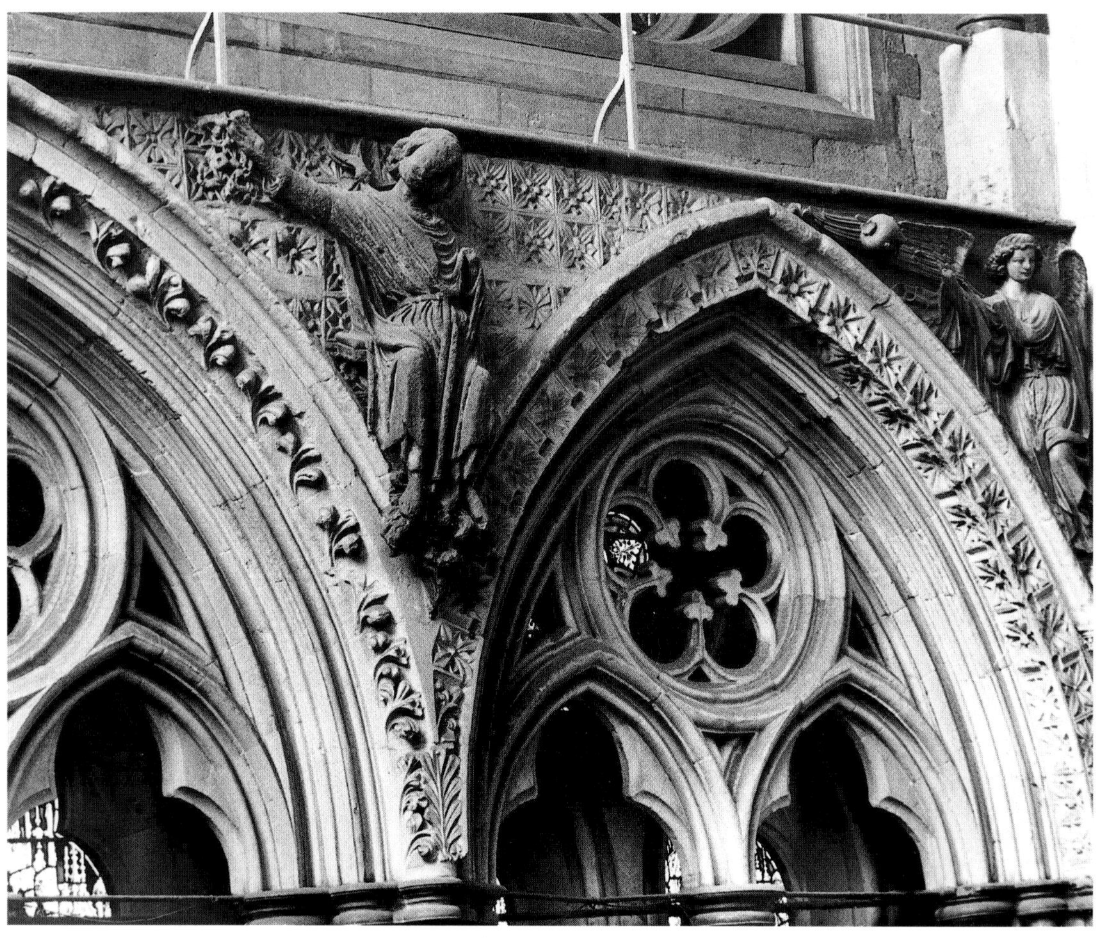

High in the triforium of Westminster Abbey, the angels filling the spandrels are among the finest examples of English mediaeval sculpture carved c.1255. Swinging censers is a typical angelic task.

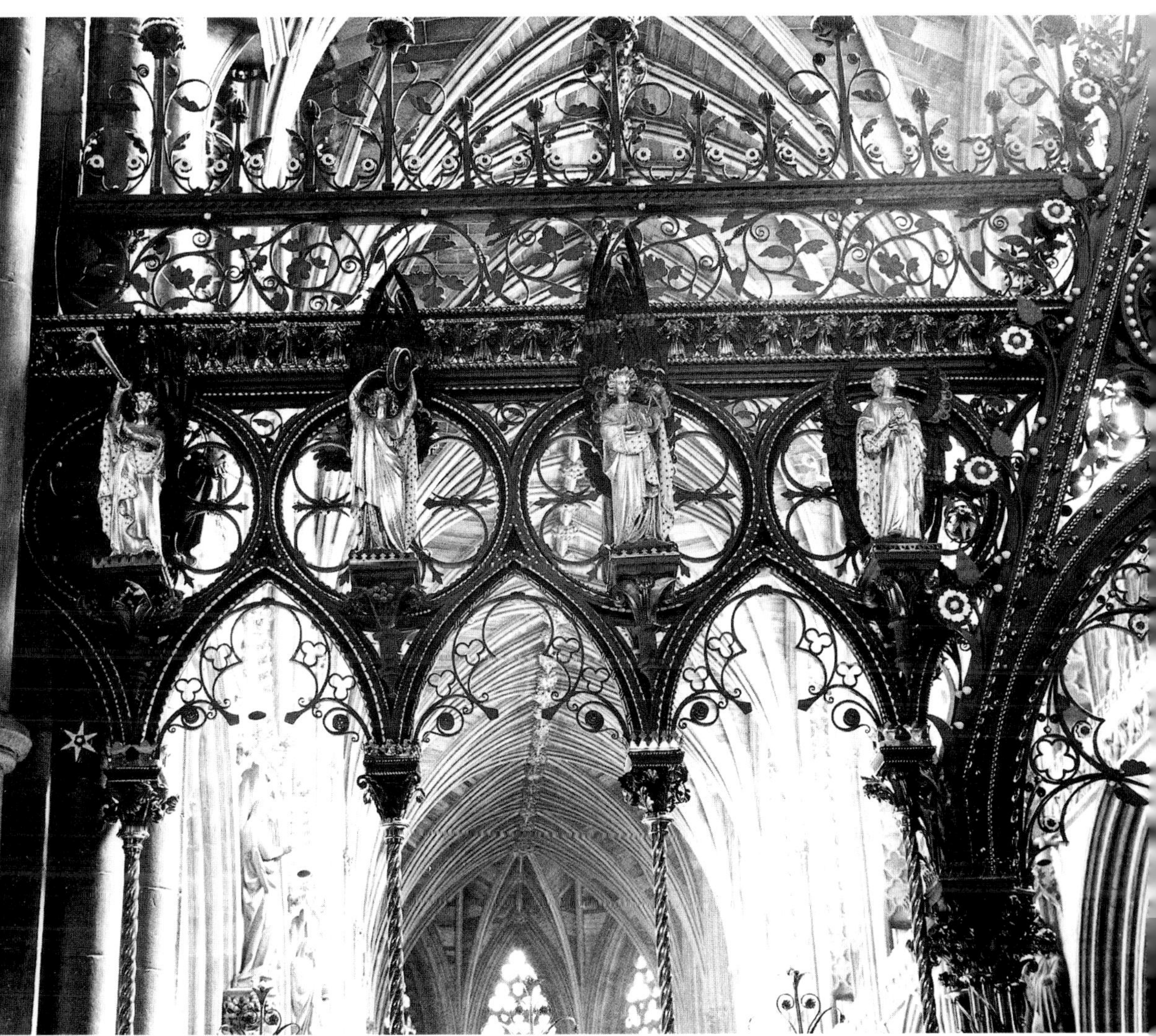

The wrought iron screen in Lichfield Cathedral was designed in 1859 by Sir George Gilbert Scott, and made by Francis Skidmore of Coventry. The angel musicians are the work of Bernie Philip.

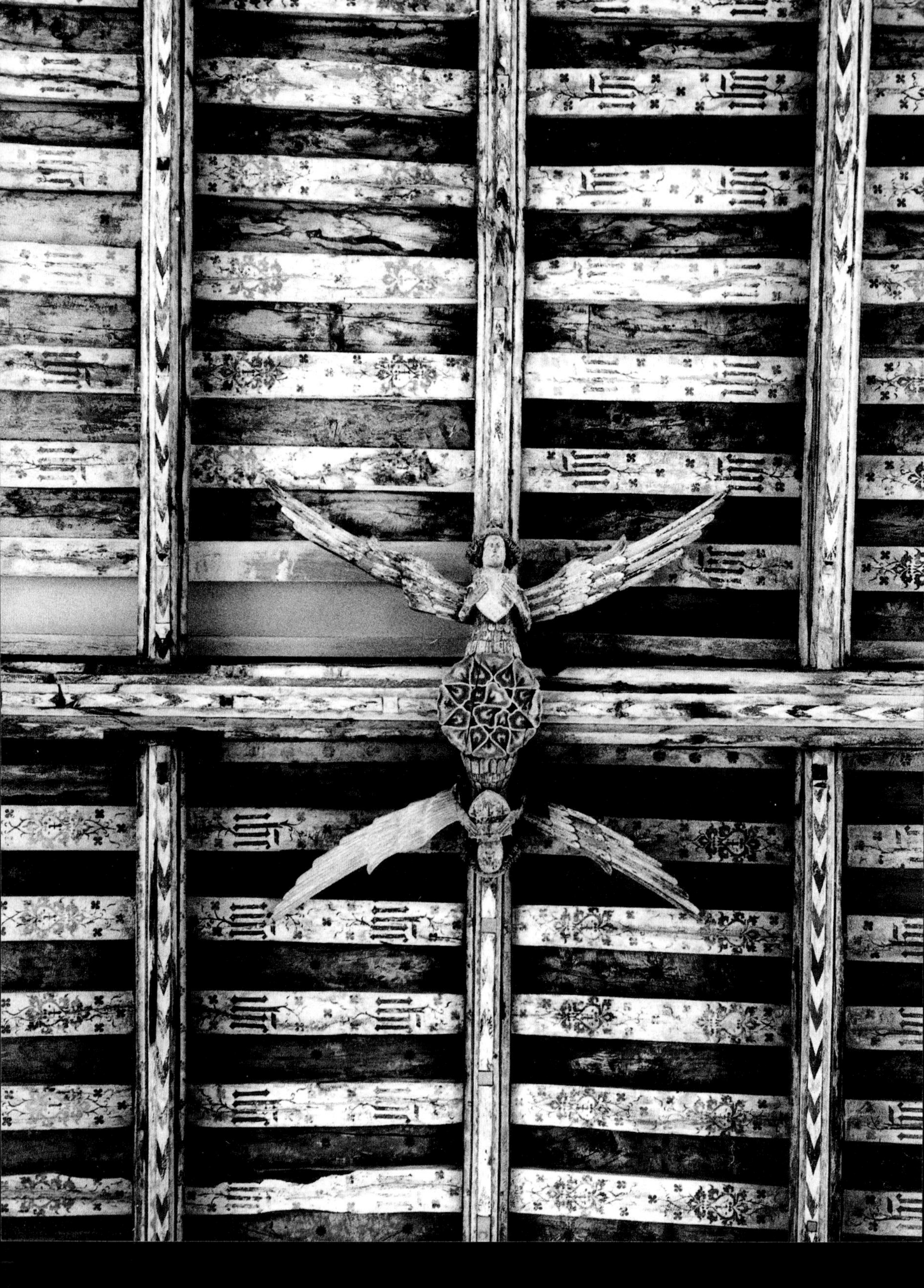

In 1499 Bishop Oliver King had a dream of angels ascending and descending ladders to Heaven, and a voice commanding 'a King to restore the church.' And so he rebuilt the crumbling west front of Bath Abbey, and included in his design two ladders with climbing angels.

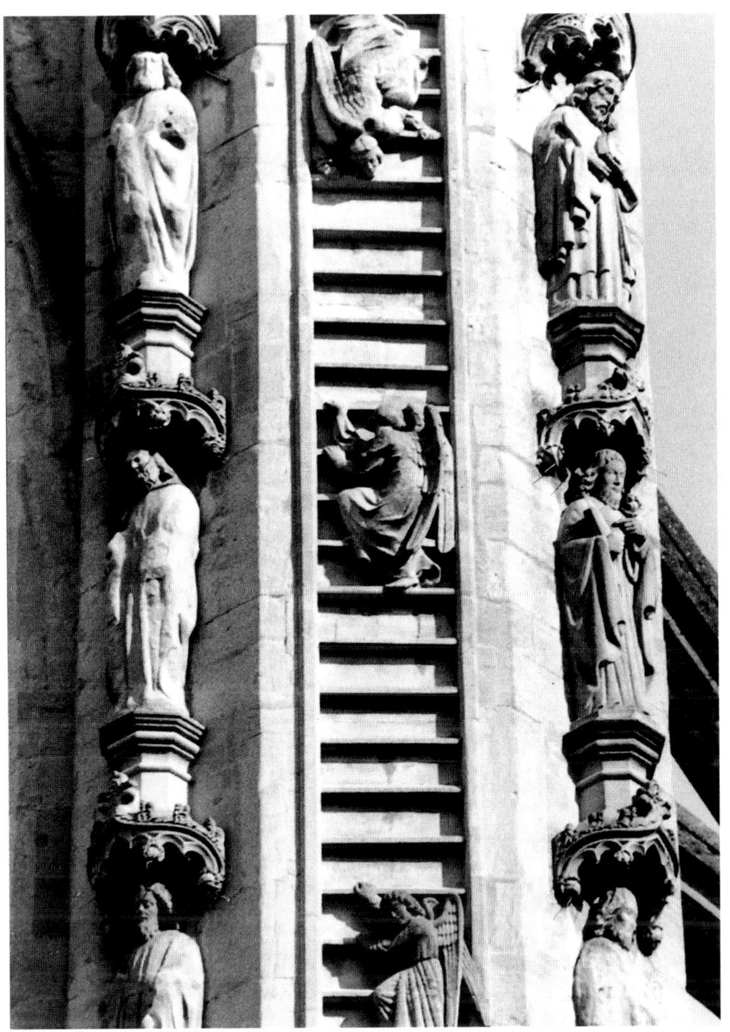

Left: William Dowsing, the infamous Parliamentary Visitor to East Anglia, was commissioned by Cromwell's Parliament to destroy 'all Monuments of Superstition'. His diaries record the destruction of over a thousand angels, although these beautiful 15th century figures on the roof of Blythburgh Church defied his best efforts: he even tried to shoot them down, and several are riddled with buckshot.

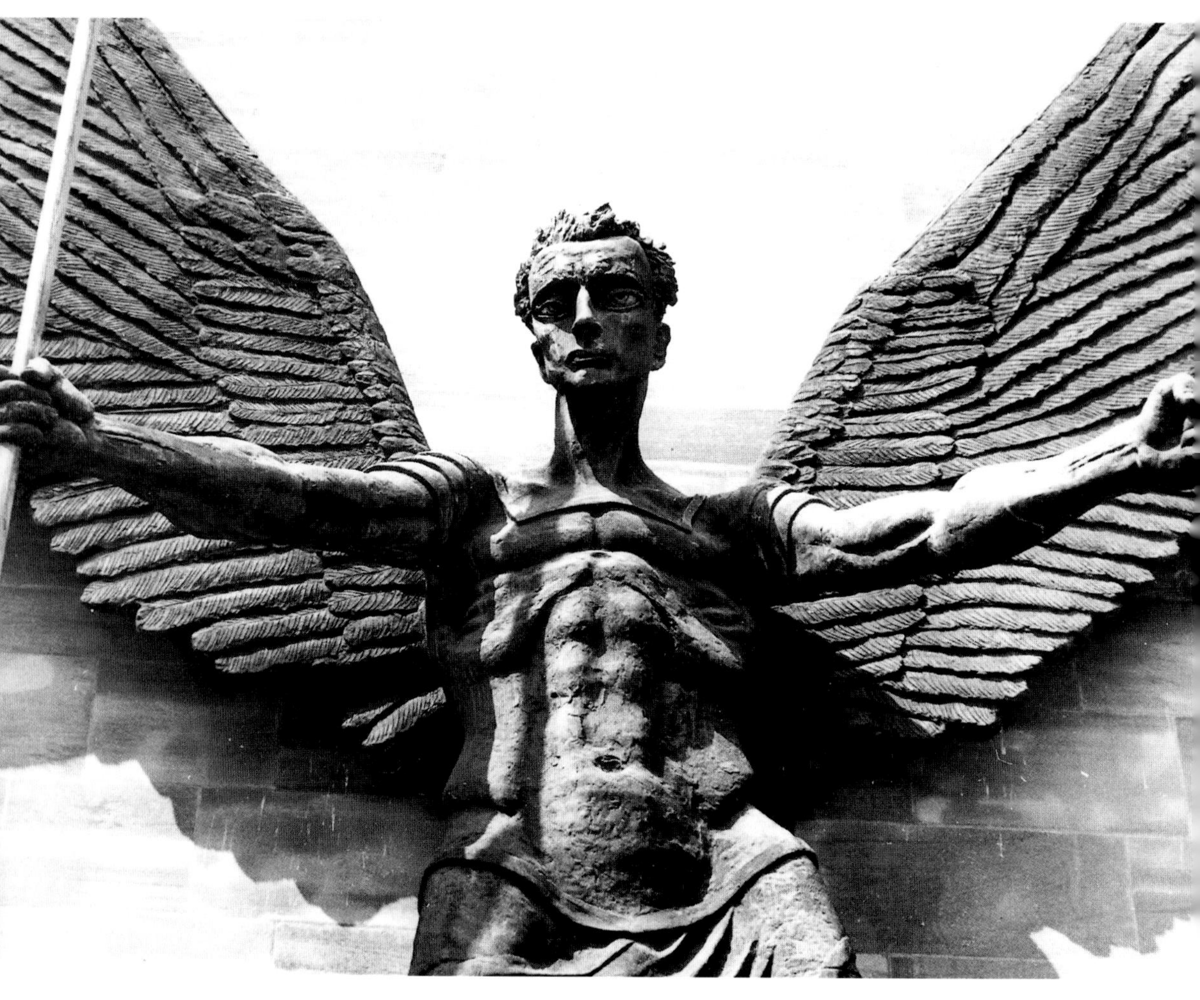

St Michael, spear in hand, triumphing over the Devil, Jacob Epstein's powerful bronze
sculpture on the south wall of the rebuilt Coventry Cathedral, consecrated in 1962.

Right: The Angel of the North, Anthony Gormley's steel sculpture with the wingspan of a jumbo jet, stands on a hillock between
the junction of the A1 and the A167, just south of Gateshead. It was financed by the local authority, and erected in 1998 after
a battle over planning permission. A lay-by enables passing motorists to stop, and many bring picnics to eat at its feet.

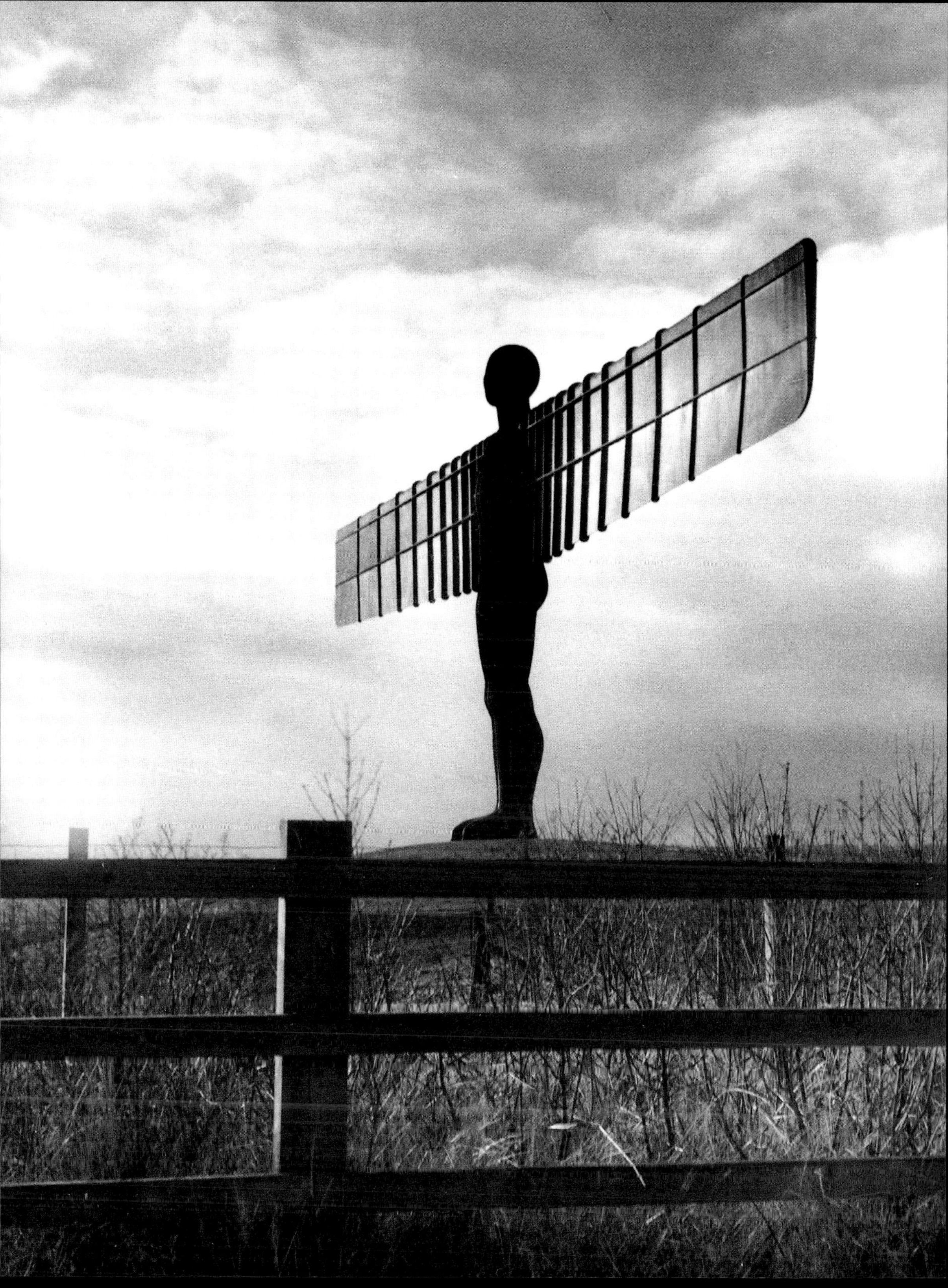

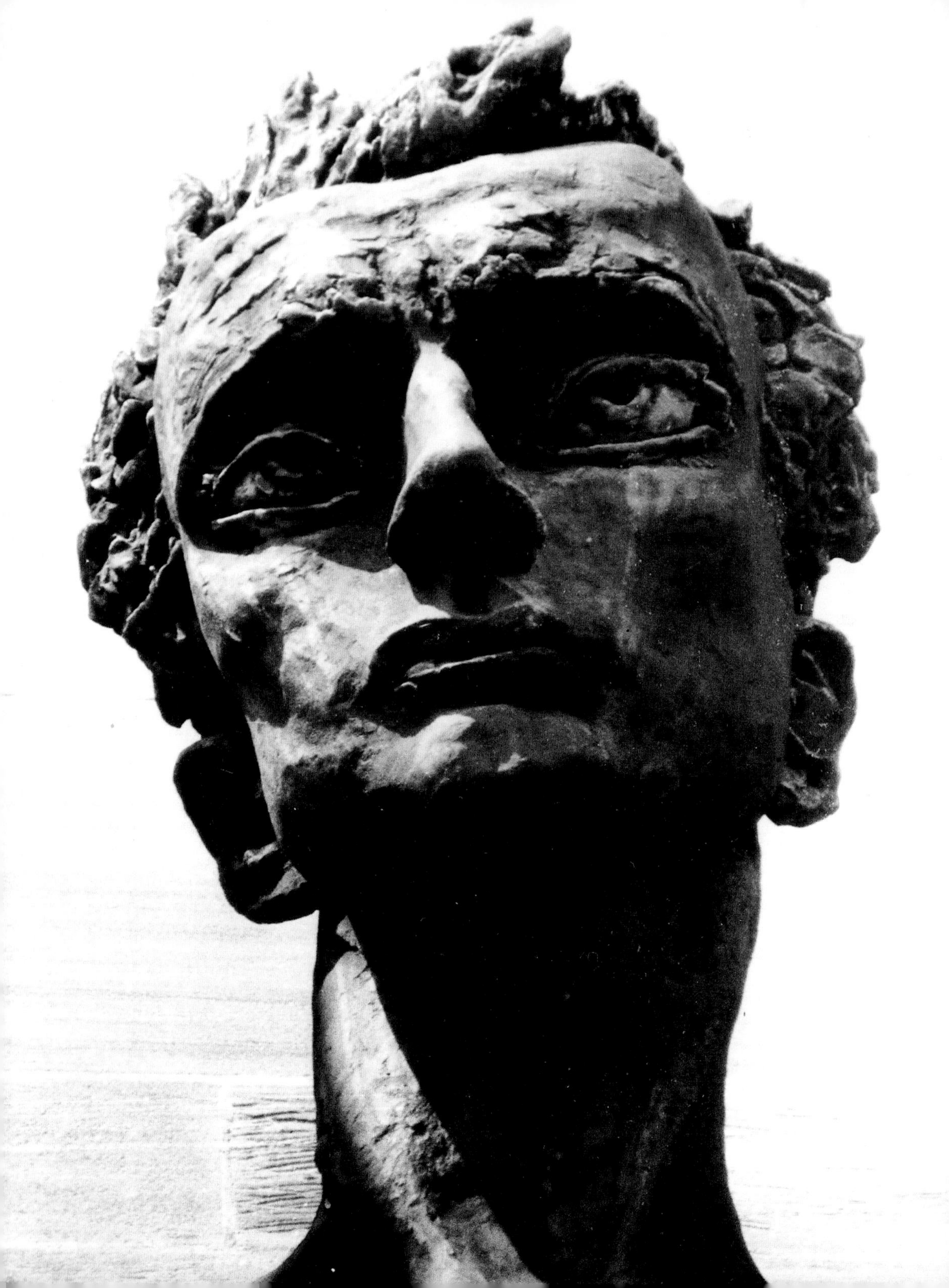

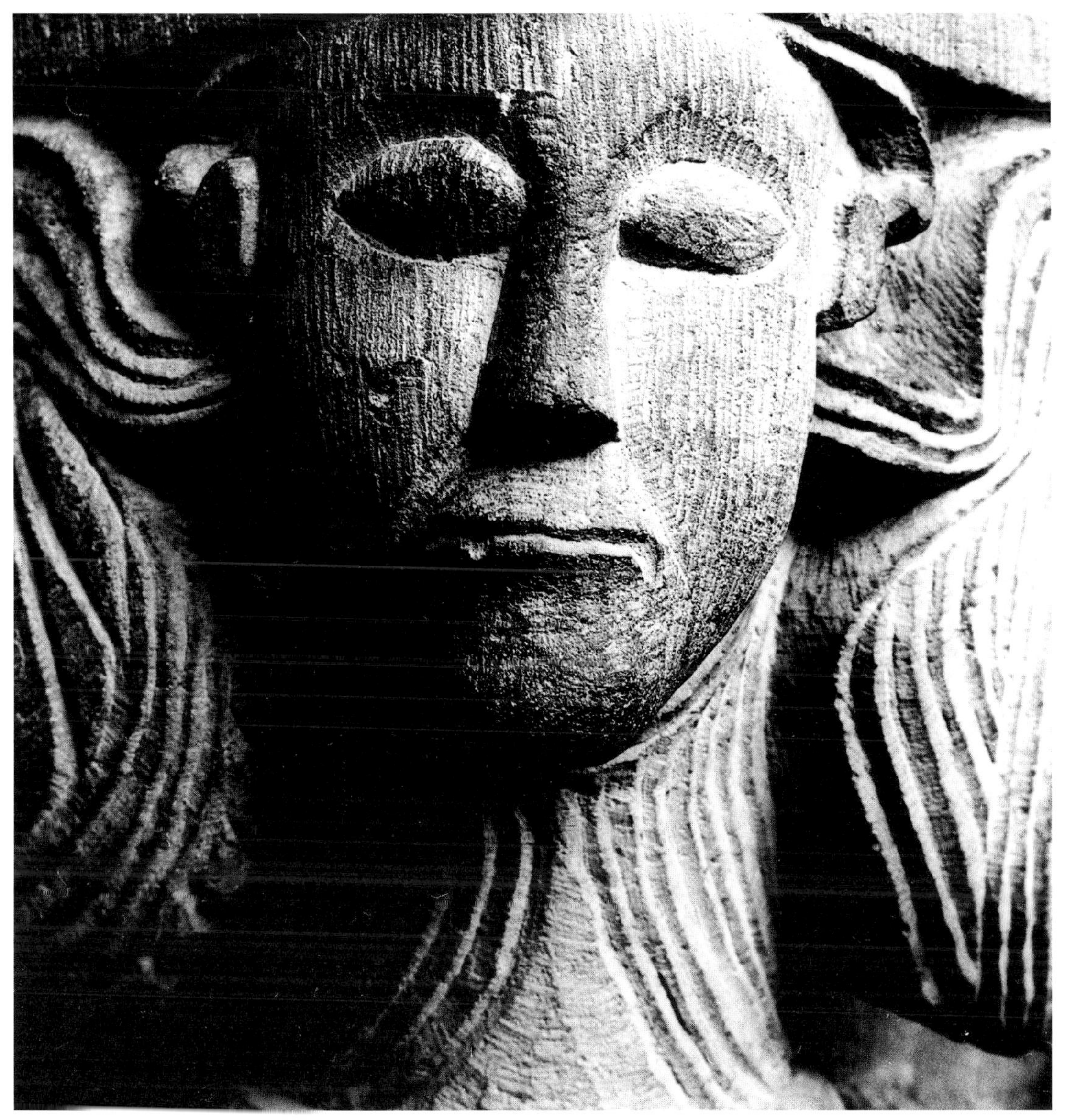

Head of an angel, on the Norman font in Bodmin church, Cornwall.

Left: Head of St Michael, Coventry Cathedral, by Jacob Epstein

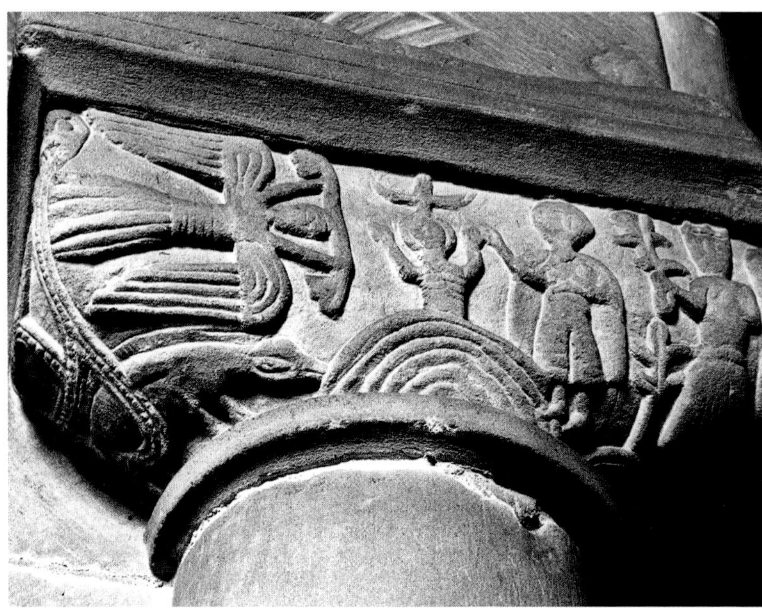

A flying angel on a Norman capital at Adel, near Leeds, holds Christ's clothes during his Baptism in the River Jordan, while the Dove of God descends.

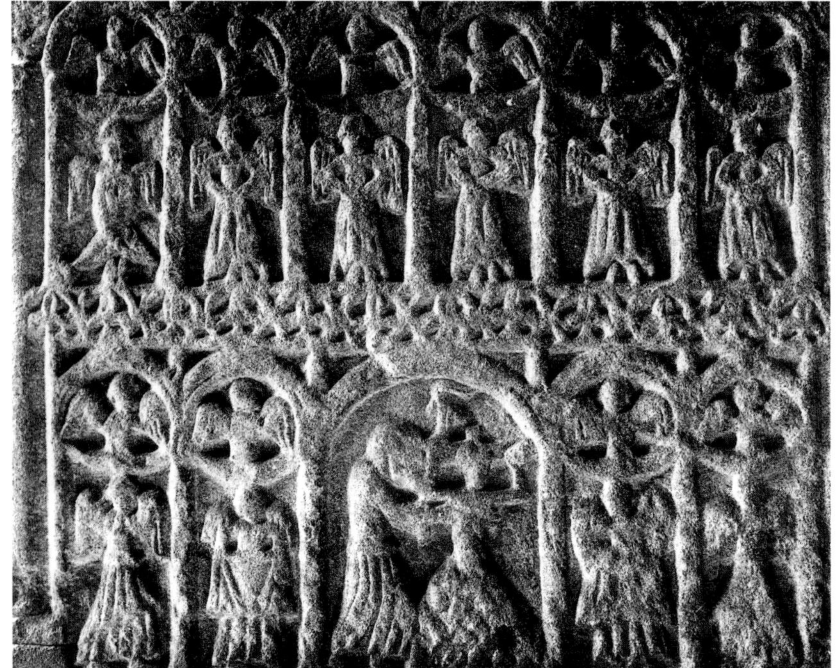

A frieze of angels on the Norman font in Lenton Priory, Nottingham.

Art Nouveau angel on the façade of Edward Everard, a Bristol printer. It is flanked by tributes to William Morris and Johannes Gutenberg, the inventor of printing.

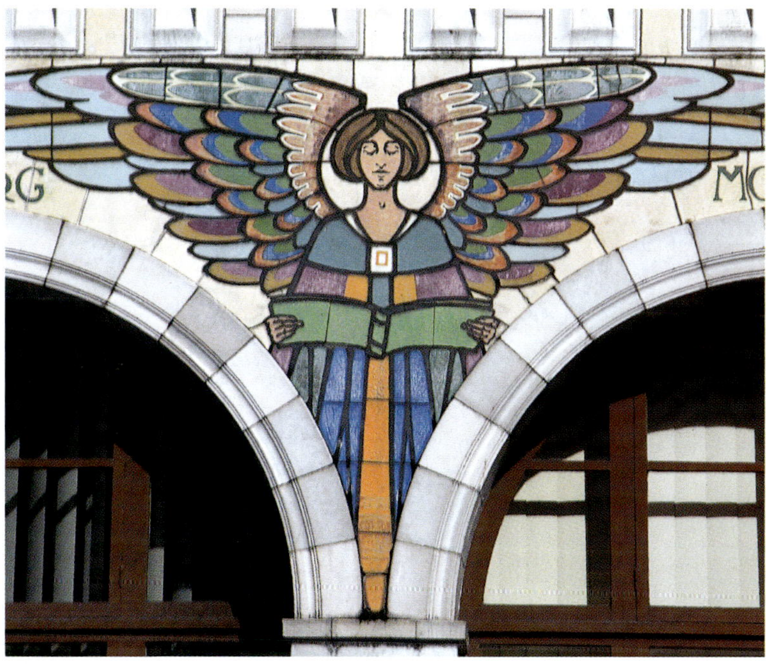

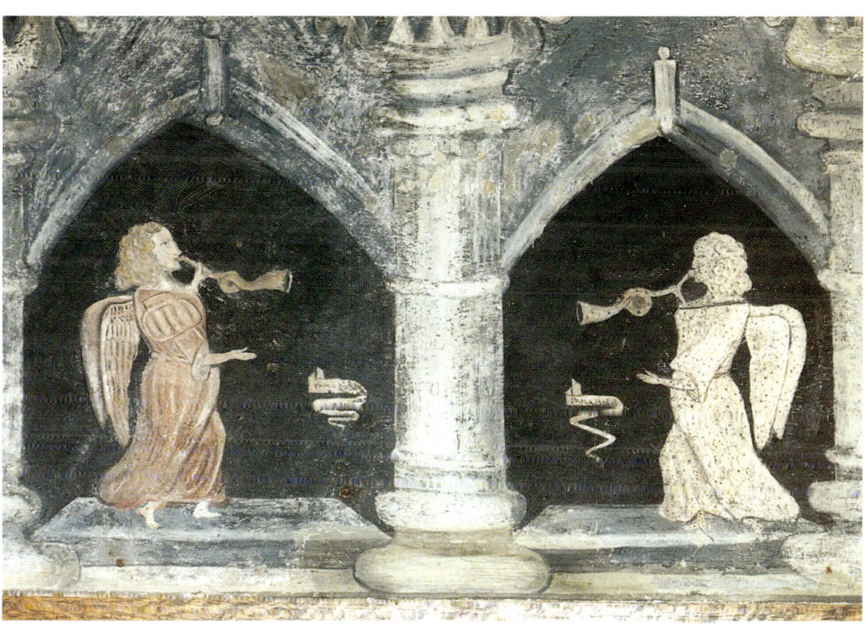

These Elizabethan angels were discovered in the 1970s above a fireplace in a solicitors' office in the little Devon town of Colyton. They represent Fama Bona and Fama Mala - Good Reputation and Bad Reputation.

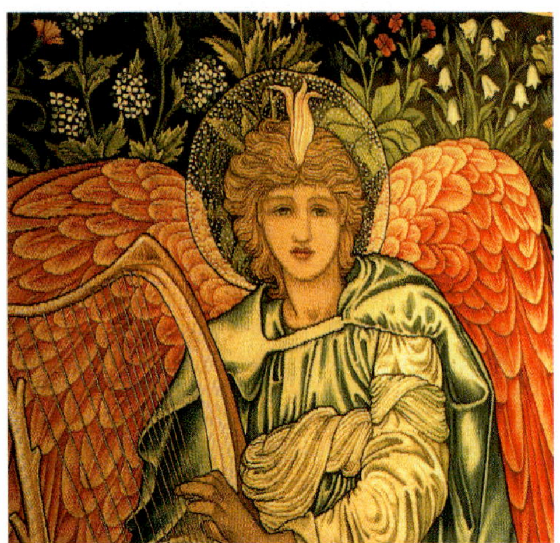

Two large tapestry angels
playing harps stand either side
of the altar at Brockhampton in
Herefordshire, an Arts and Crafts
church by W. R. Lethaby. They
were designed by Burne-Jones
and woven by Morris & Co.

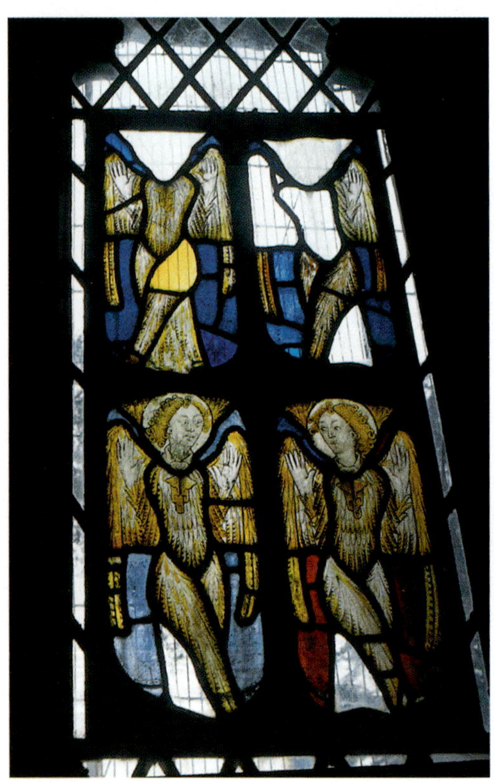

15th century glass at Lydlinch in Dorset, with feather-clad angels.

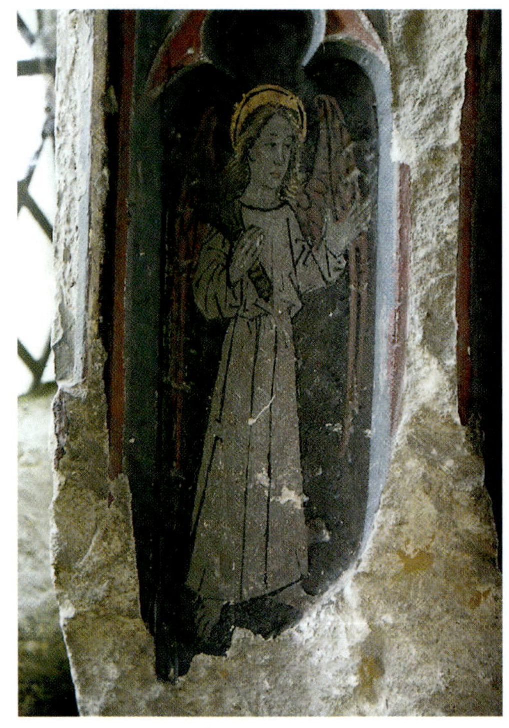

This carved stone panel, painted with angels, probably
came from Hailes Abbey, but now sits on a window
sill in the church at Buckland, Gloucestershire.

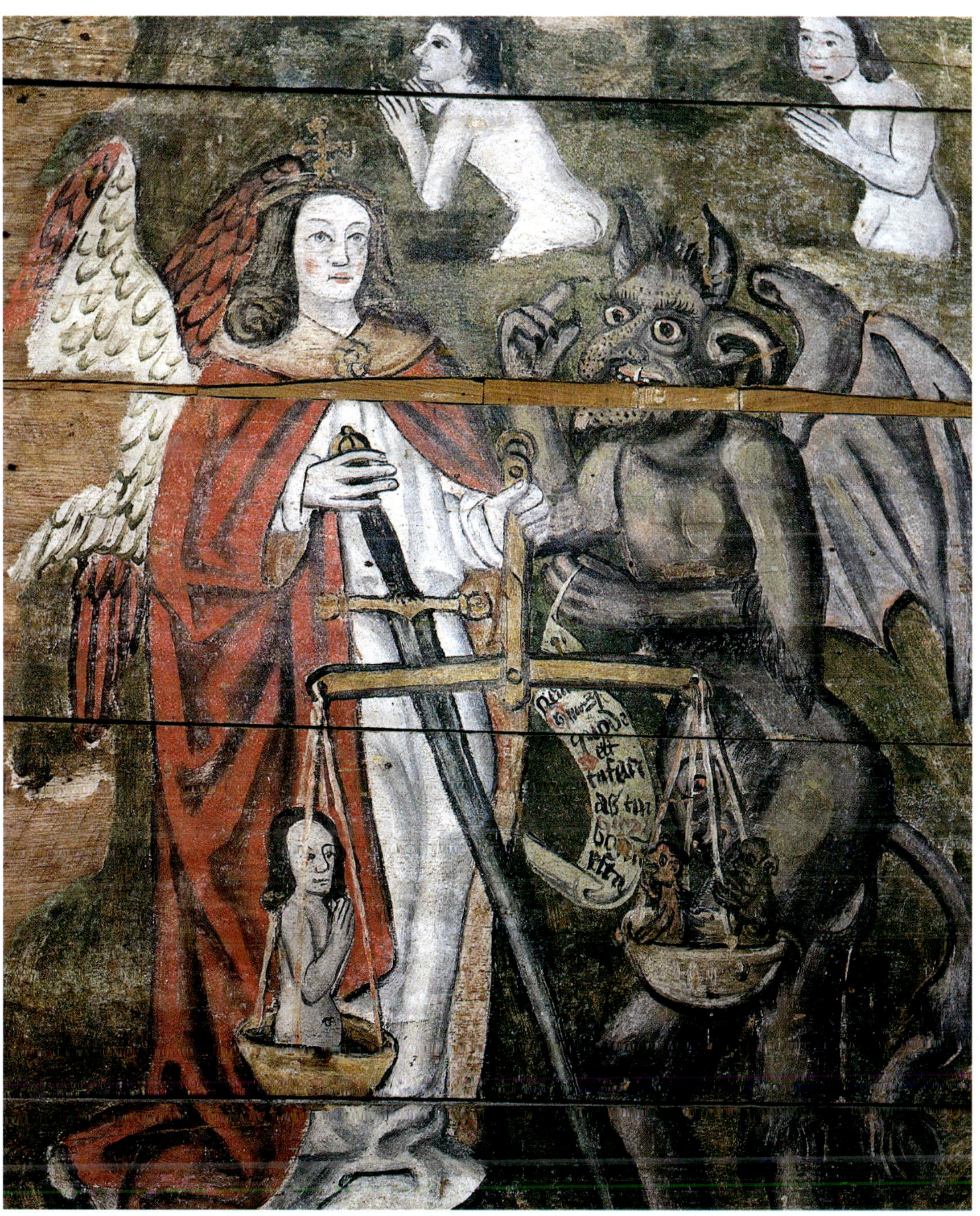

St Michael weighs the souls, while the Devil waits for the sinners, in a Doom painting on wooden boards at Wenhaston in Suffolk. Hidden for centuries by whitewash, it was thrown out into the churchyard in 1892, when it was washed by a miraculous shower of rain, to the horror of the sexton.

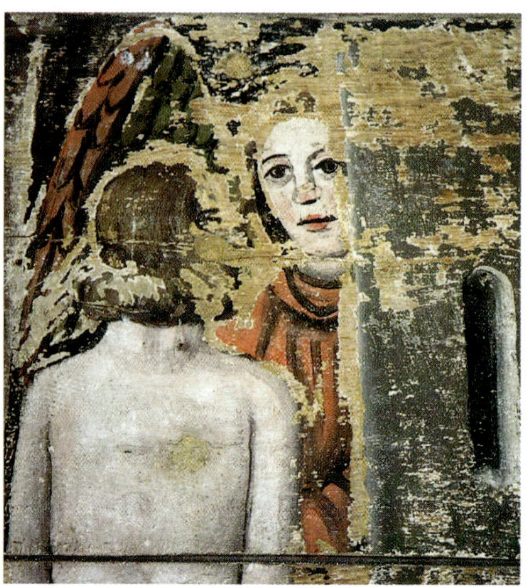

An angel admits one of the saved to
Heaven from the Wenhaston Doom.

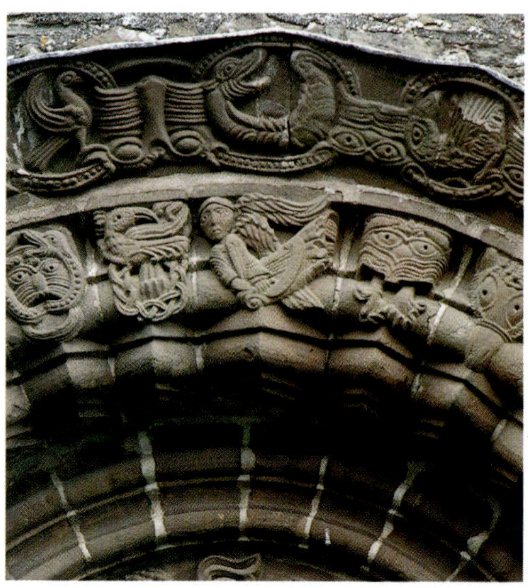

An angel flying amongst birds and mythical beasts,
in the fantastical carvings around the doorway of
Kilpeck, one of the great series of sculptures by the
Hereford school of craftsmen in the mid-12th century.

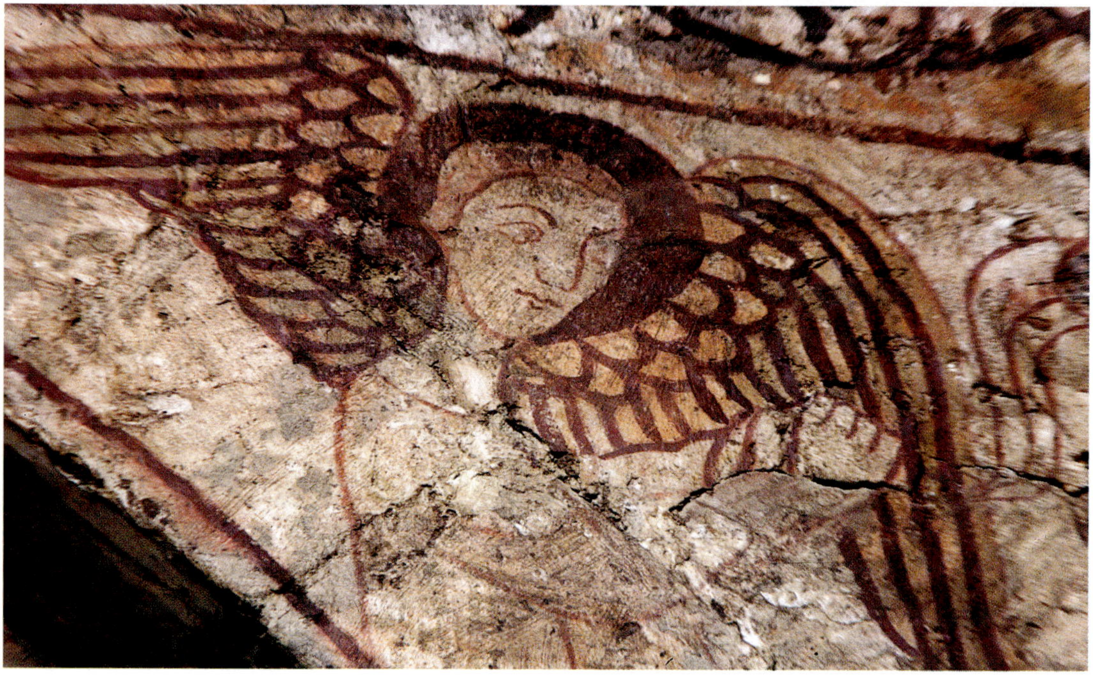

The wall paintings from Claverley in Shropshire date from 1200, and were rediscovered in 1902.

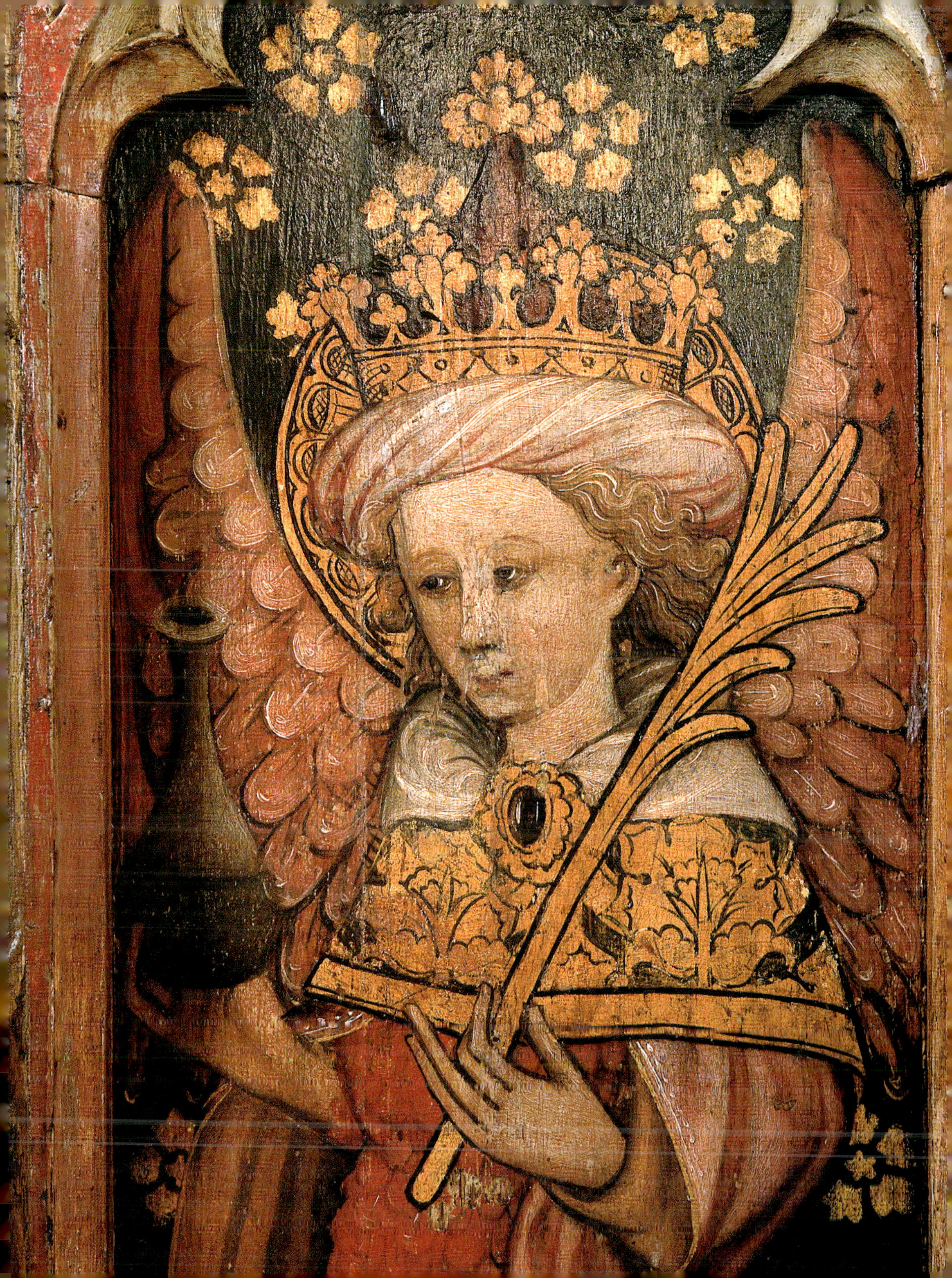

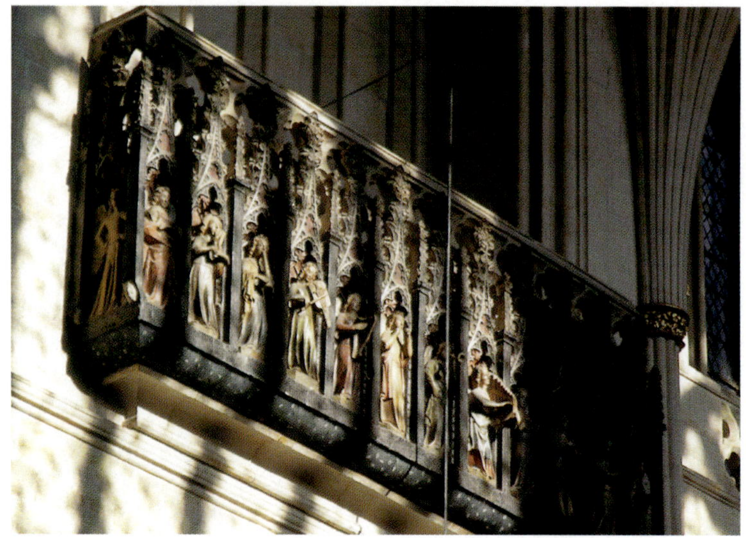

The Minstrels' Gallery, Exeter Cathedral, which dates from the 1360s. The angels are playing (from left to right): citole, bagpipes, recorder, mediaeval fiddle, harp, a missing (blown) instrument, short trumpet, portative organ, gittern, shawm, tambourine, and cymbals.

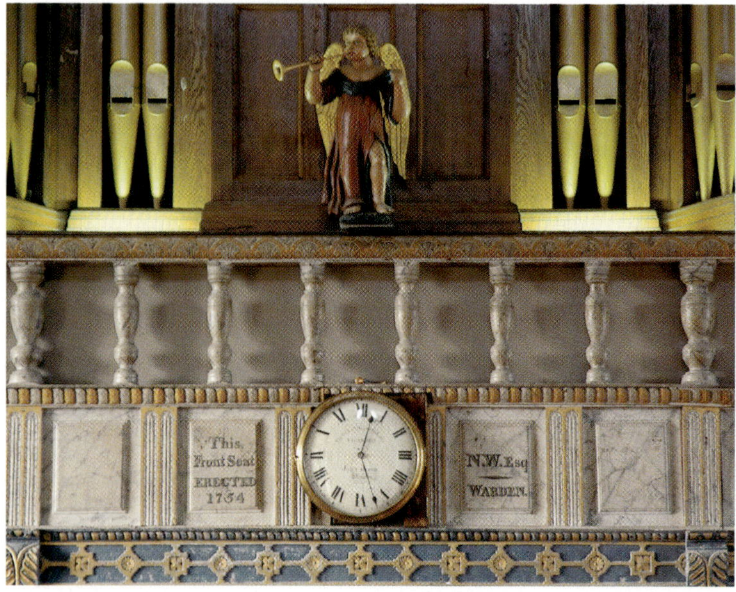

The angel on the west gallery at Sidbury in Devon comes originally from the sounding board of the pulpit. West galleries were for musicians to perform while accompanying the hymns, and many were demolished when the musicians were replaced by organs. In this case the organ was placed in the gallery, and the angel stands in for the missing players.

Previous page: Detail of the 15th century painted screen at Barton Turf in Norfolk, which shows the nine orders of angels. This is Principatus, protector of the Kingdoms of Earth, bearing a palm frond.

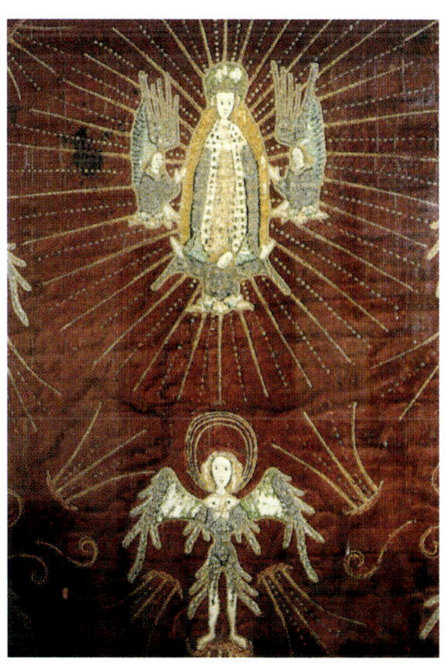

The Careby cope, embroidered in the 14th century, was later cut up for use as an altar frontal, and is now displayed in the Lincolnshire church. This detail shows an angel with Christ in Glory. The angel is remarkably similar to the one on the Culmstock cope on page 3.

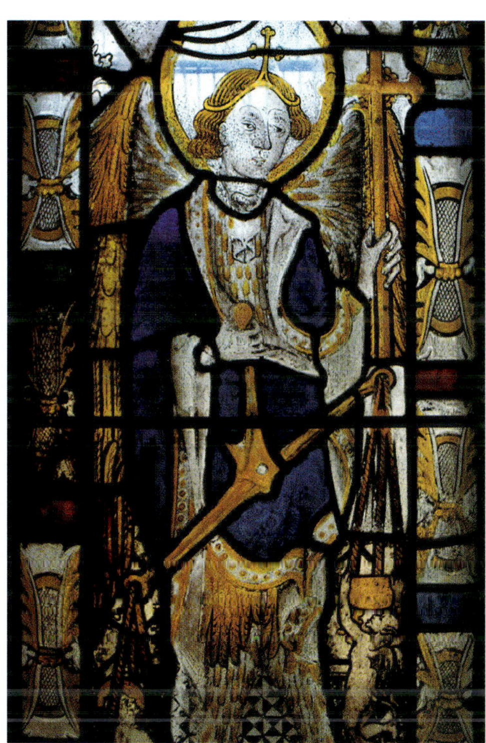

St Michael with his scales on Judgement Day, in 15th century stained glass at Doddiscombsleigh in Devon.

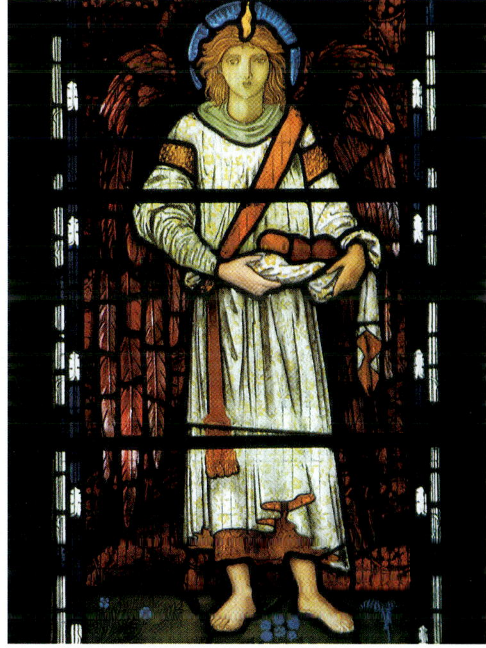

St Martin's in Scarborough is an early church by the great Victorian architect G. F. Bodley, and he commissioned all the decorations from the young Pre-Raphaelites. This angel window was the combined work of William Morris, Burne-Jones and Philip Webb.

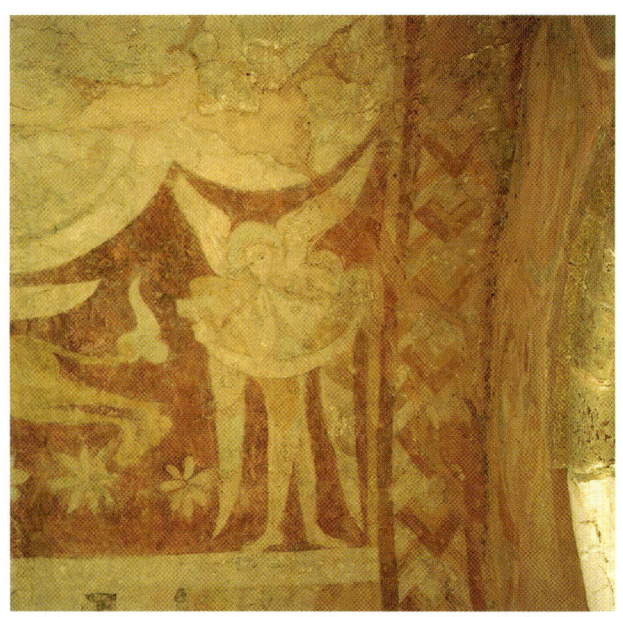

A seraphim with its six wings, from the remarkable wall paintings at Kempley in Gloucestershire, surviving from as early as 1130-40. Whitewashed in the Reformation, they were rediscovered in 1872.

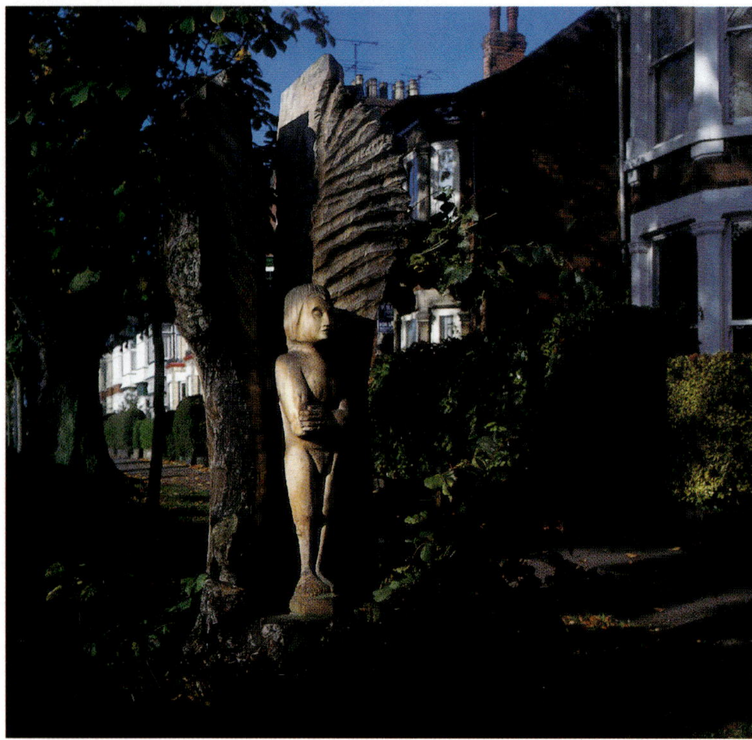

Angel carved from a lime tree by Kevin Storch, Marlborough Avenue, Hull, 1990s.

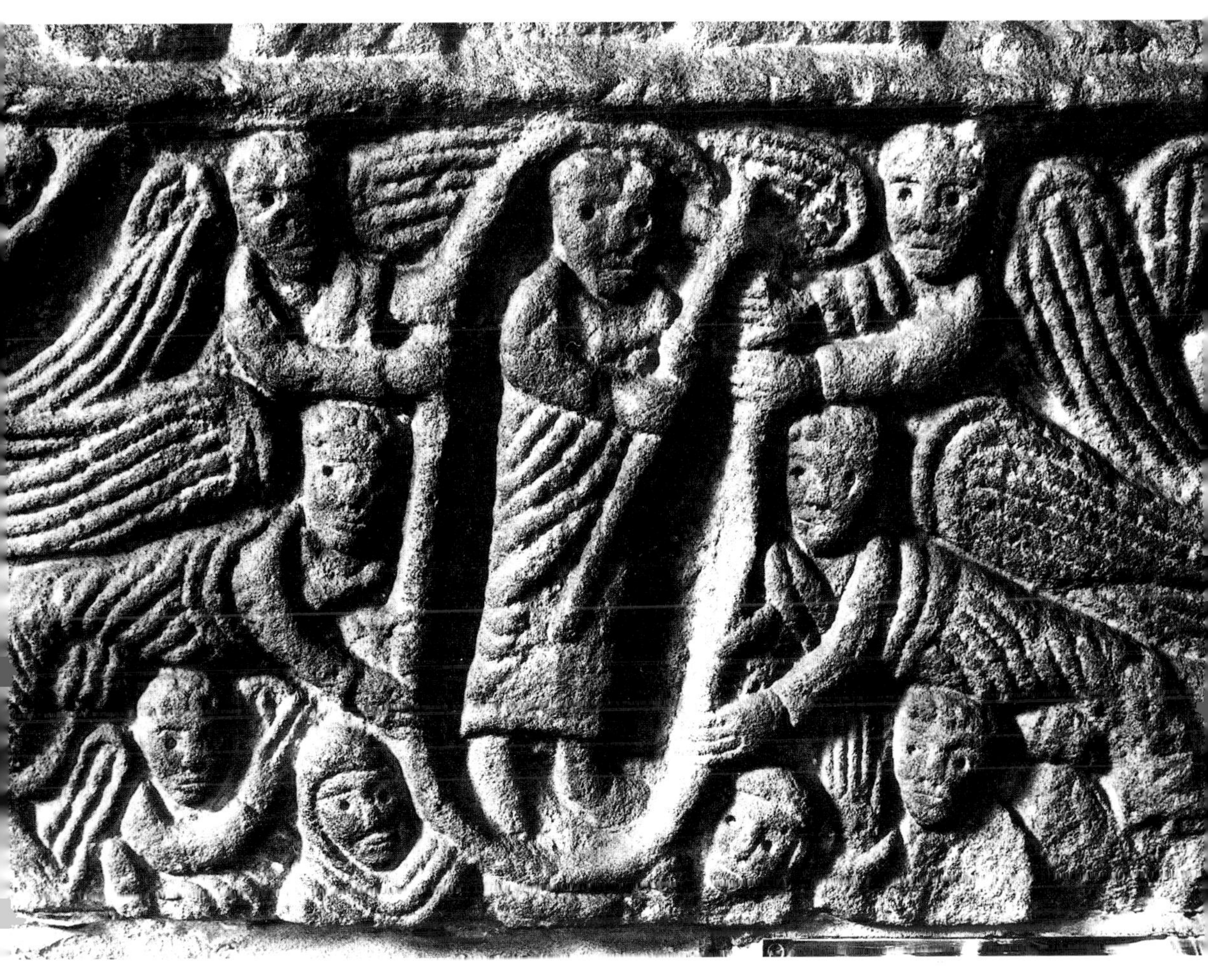

Saxon carving from the lid of a tombchest, Wirksworth, Derbyshire.

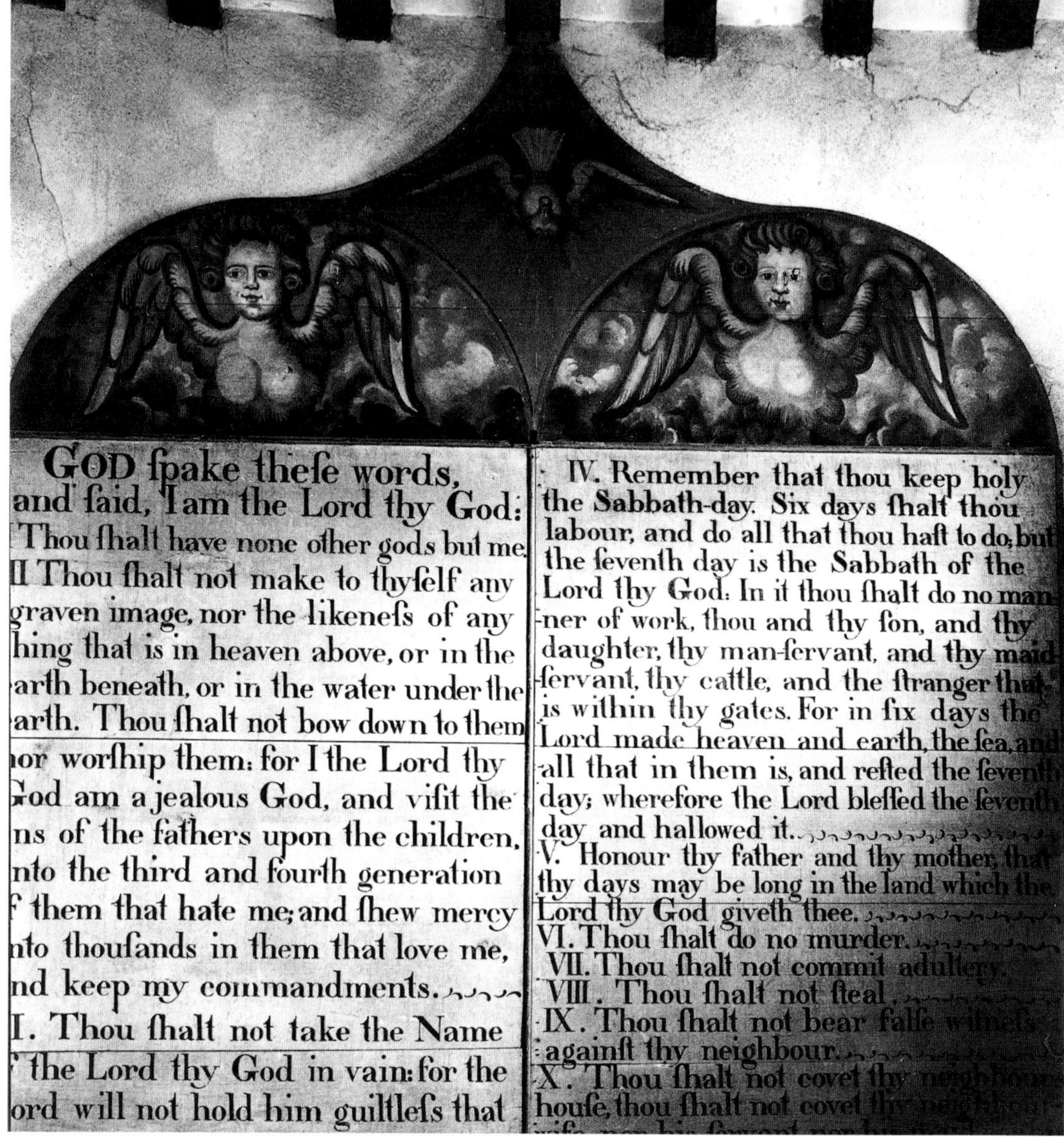

17th century Commandment Board in the church at Cartmel Fell, Cumbria. Elizabeth I ordered that the Royal Arms and boards inscribed with the ten commandments should be placed in every church, partly to redecorate the interiors which had been stripped of much of their ornament (including angels) by fanatical Puritan iconoclasts at the Reformation.

Right: This angel on a shop in Stonegate in York was originally carved in the 17th century for the forecastle of a ship.

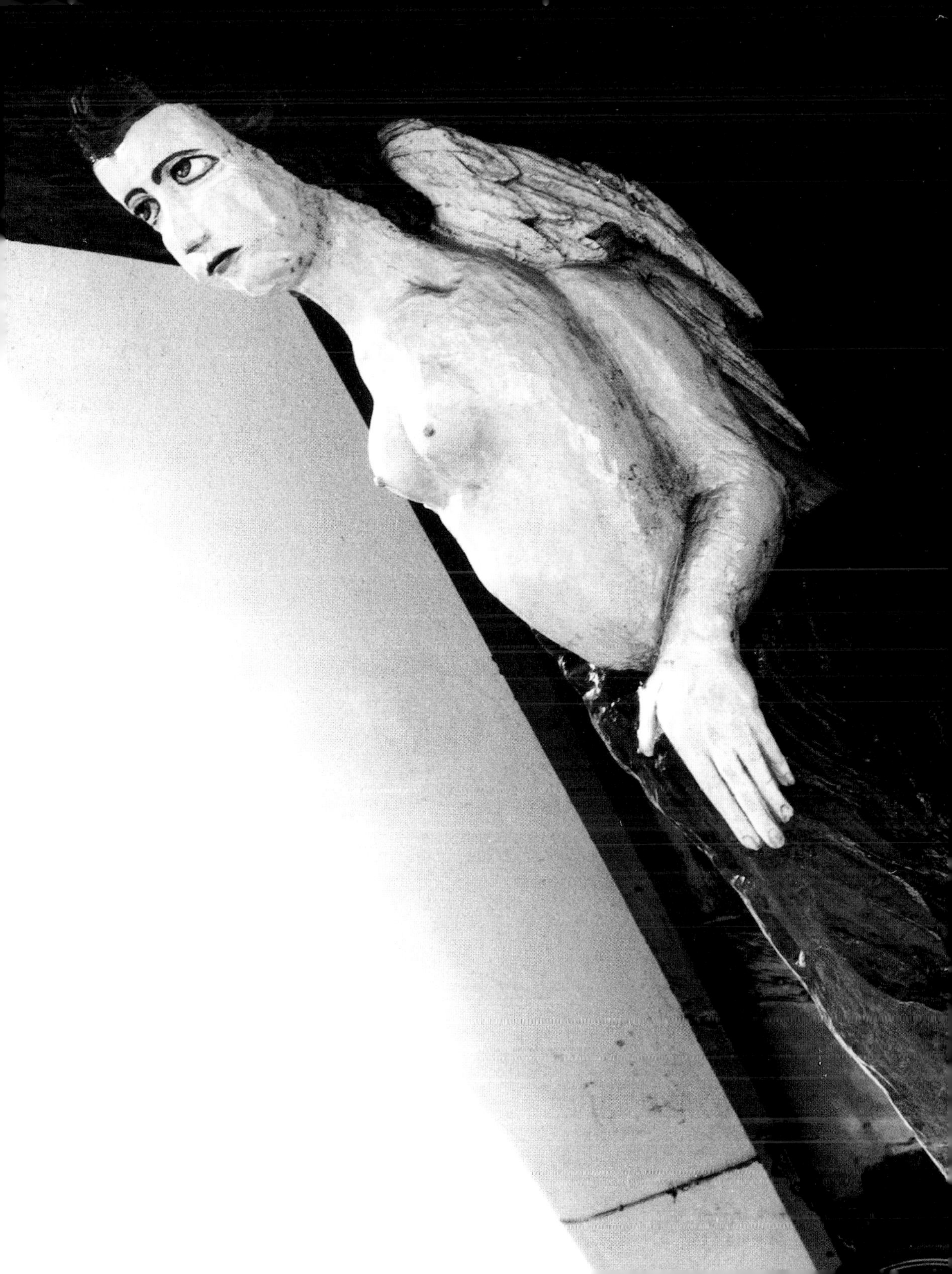

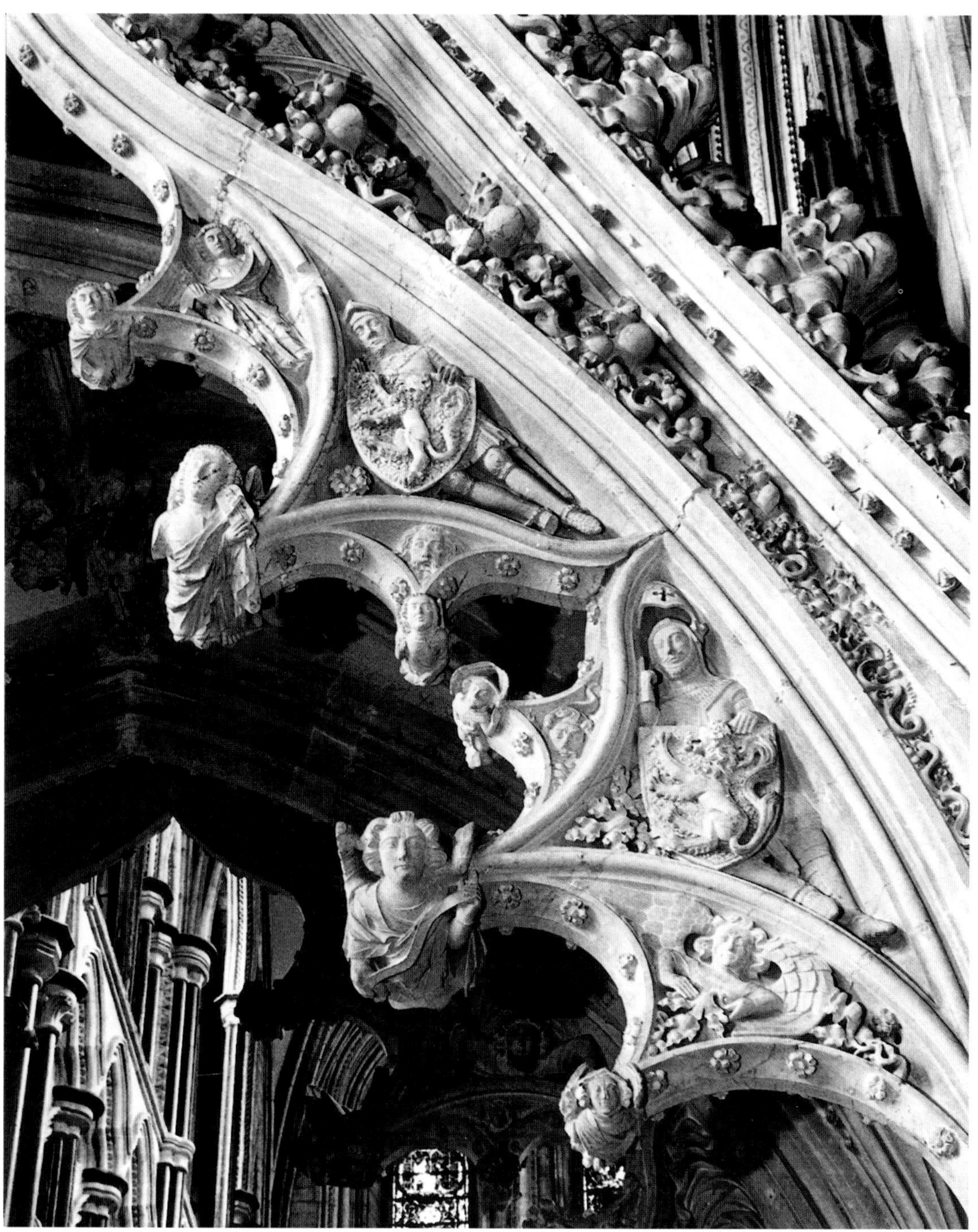

The Percy tomb in Beverley Minster, with its flights of finely sculpted angels,
is that of an unknown member of the once powerful Northumbrian family.

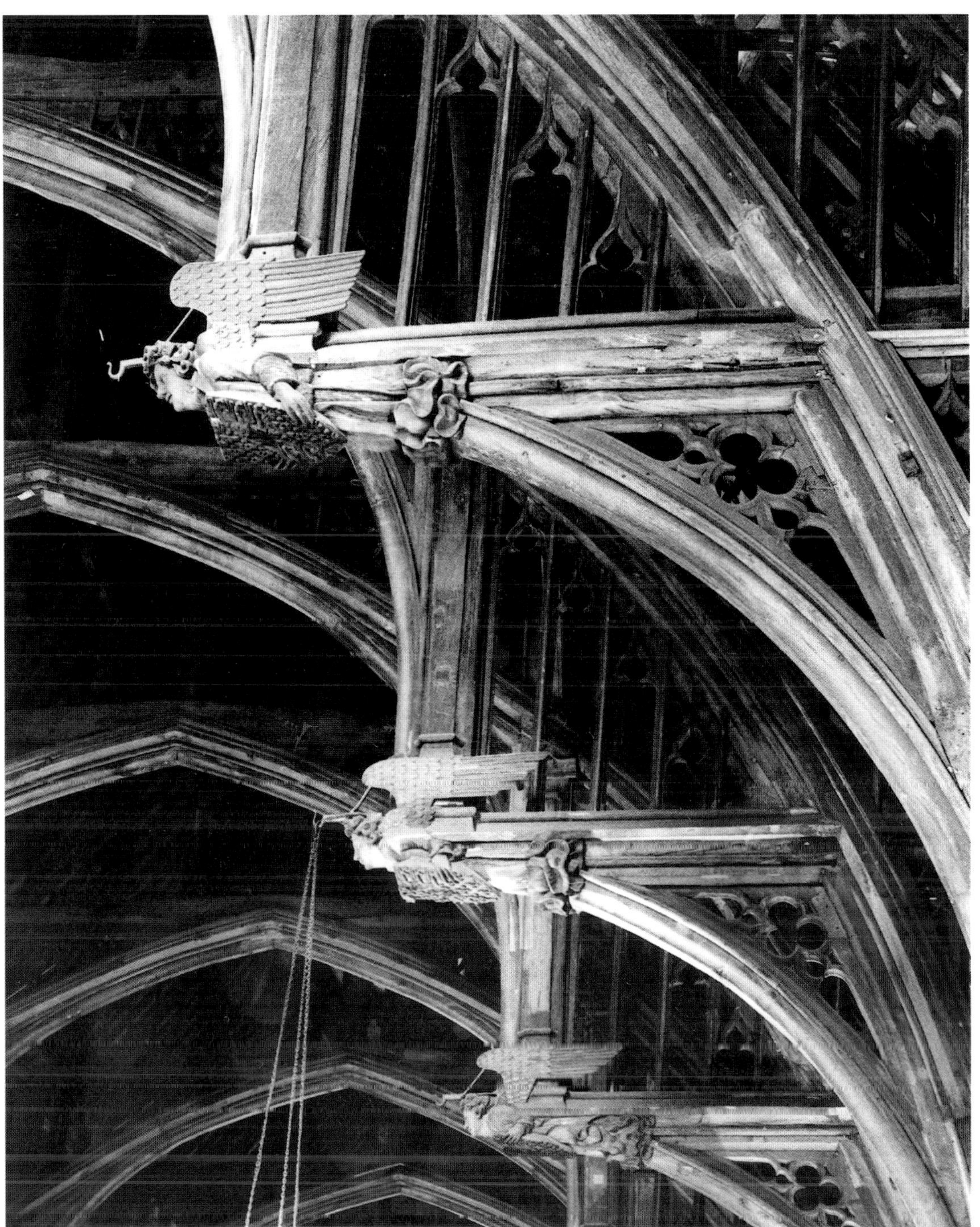

The angels in the hammerbeam roof of Westminster Hall were commissioned by Richard II, whose arms they bear, in 1398, at a cost of 27 shillings per angel. No sooner were they installed than they witnessed his deposition by Henry Bolingbroke in this very hall.

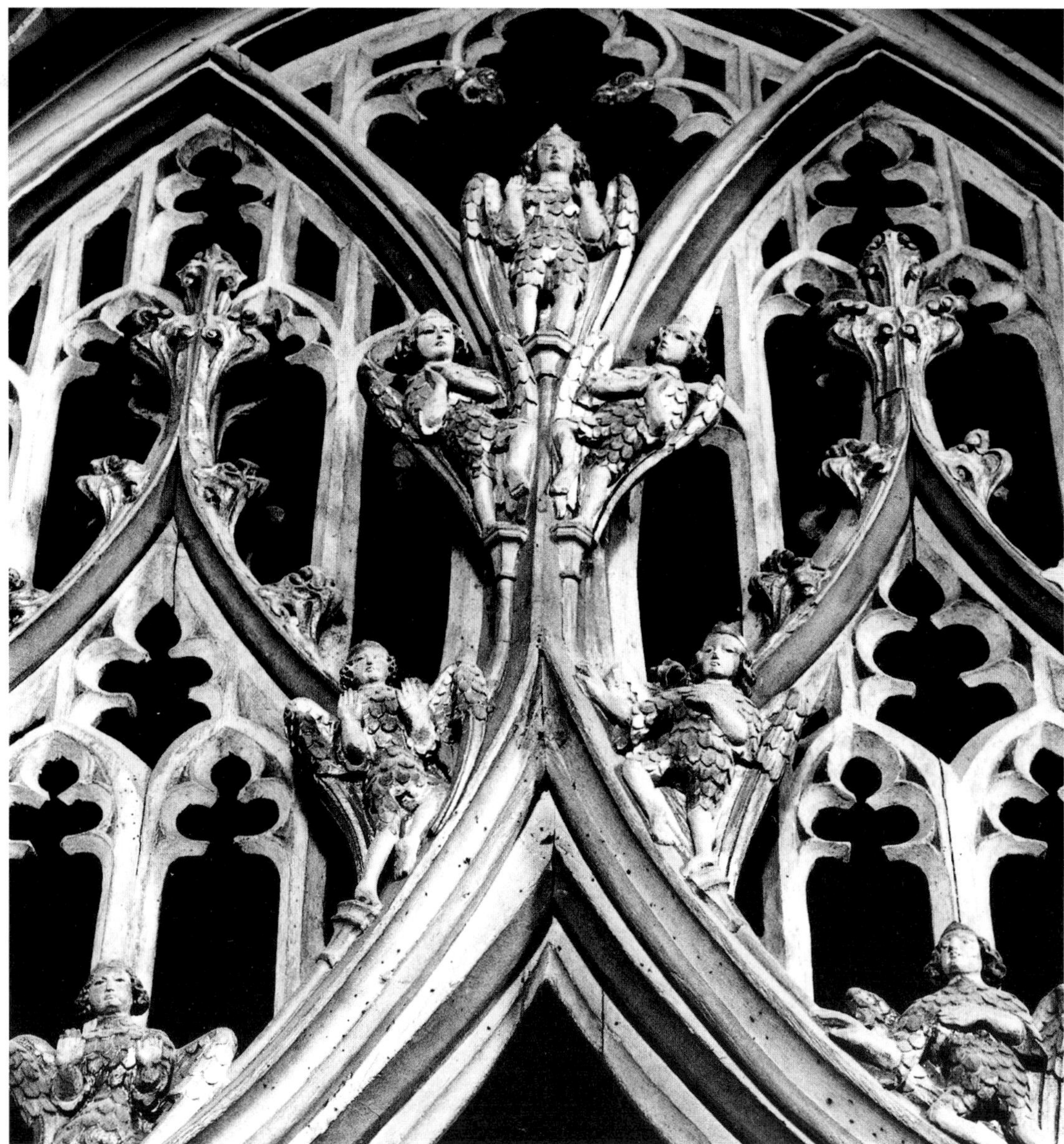

The 15th century chancel screen at Felmersham in Bedfordshire
provides a resting place for these feathered angels.

Right: Wooden angel in the Jacobean baroque
chapel on the Rhug estate near Corwen.

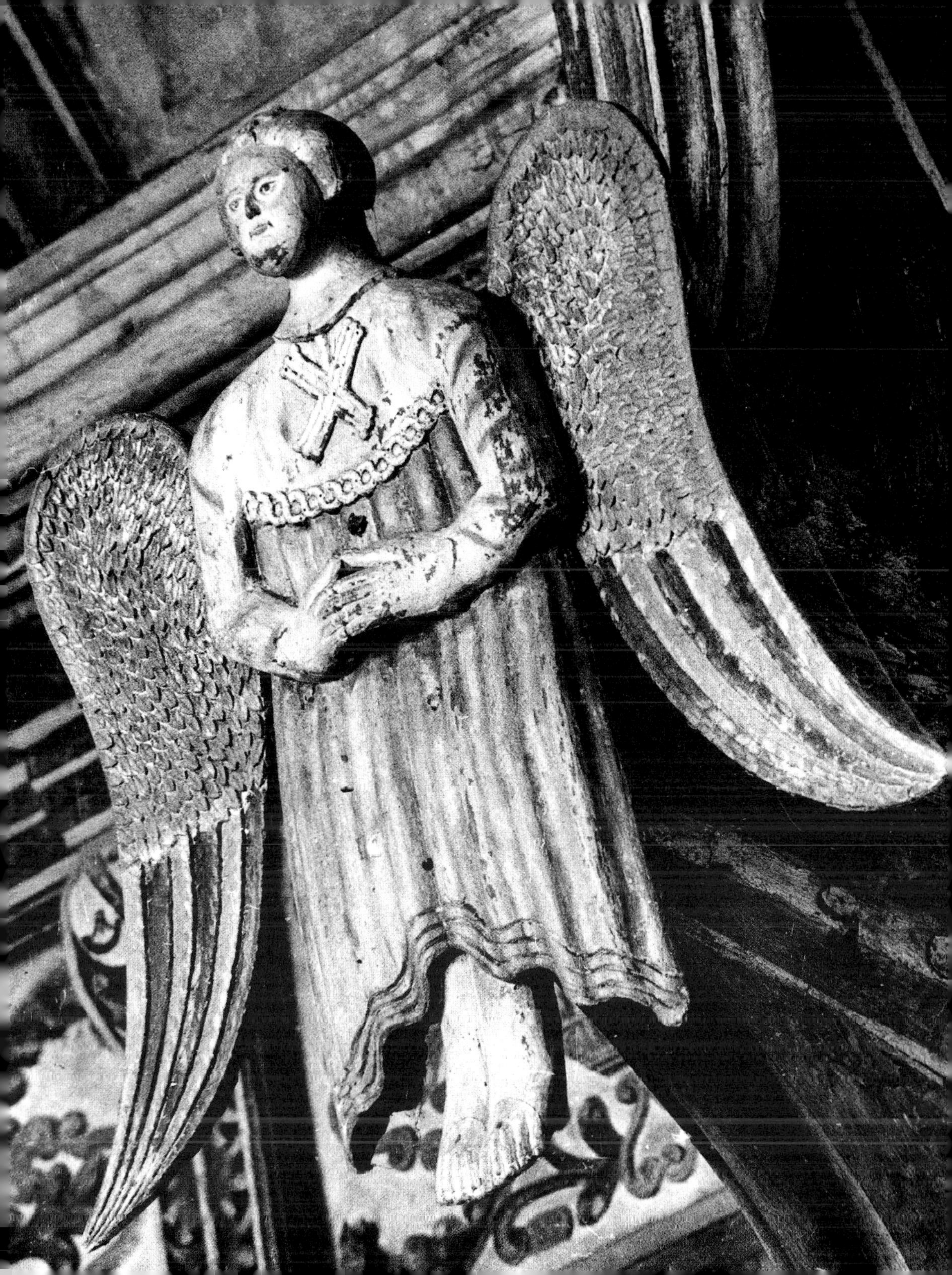

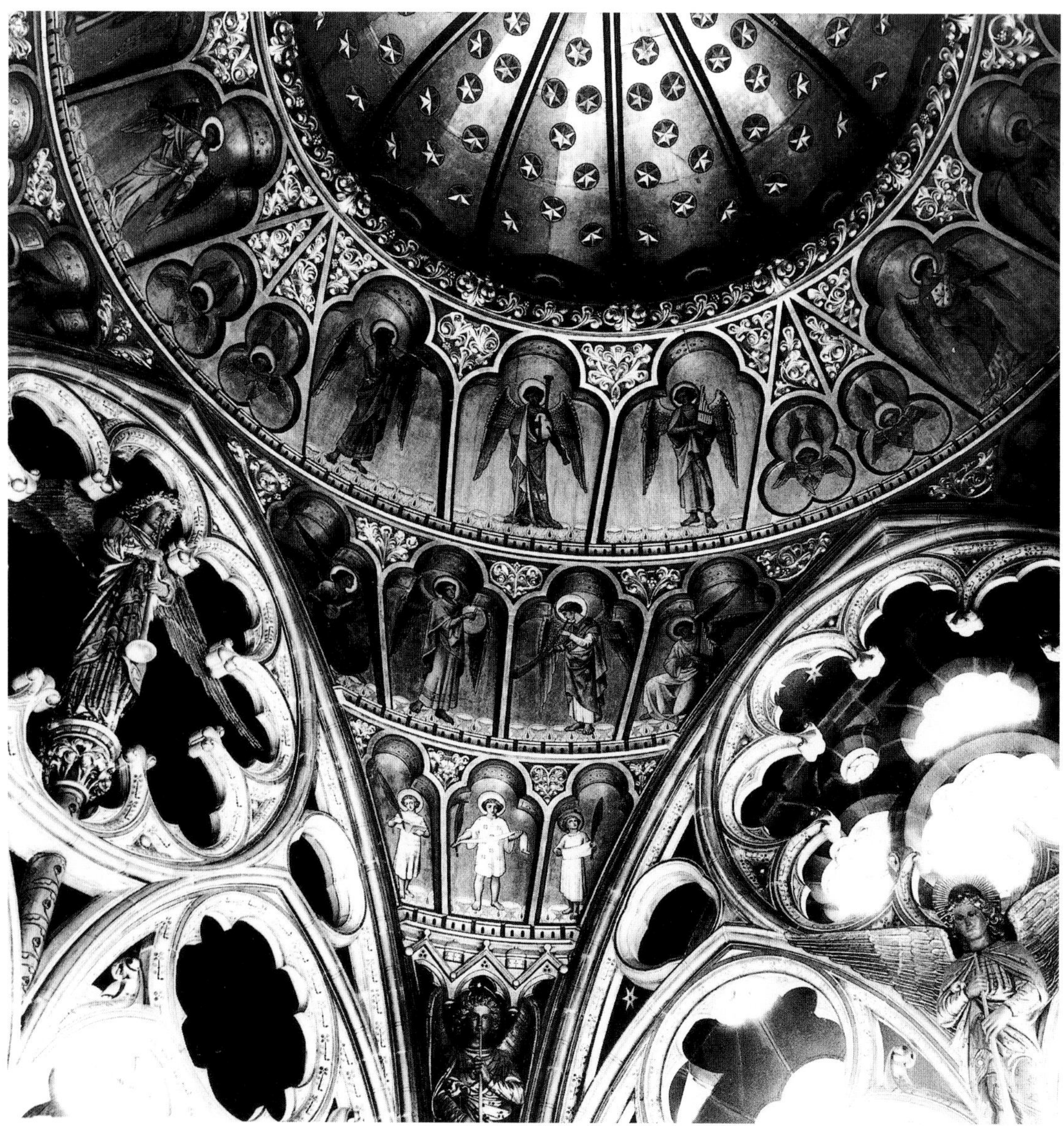

The apse of the church at Studley Royal, on the Fountains Abbey
estate in Yorkshire, decorated by its architect William Burges with
a band of High Victorian angels. A row of parrots perch below.

Right: 17th century painted ceiling in the church at Muchelney, Somerset.

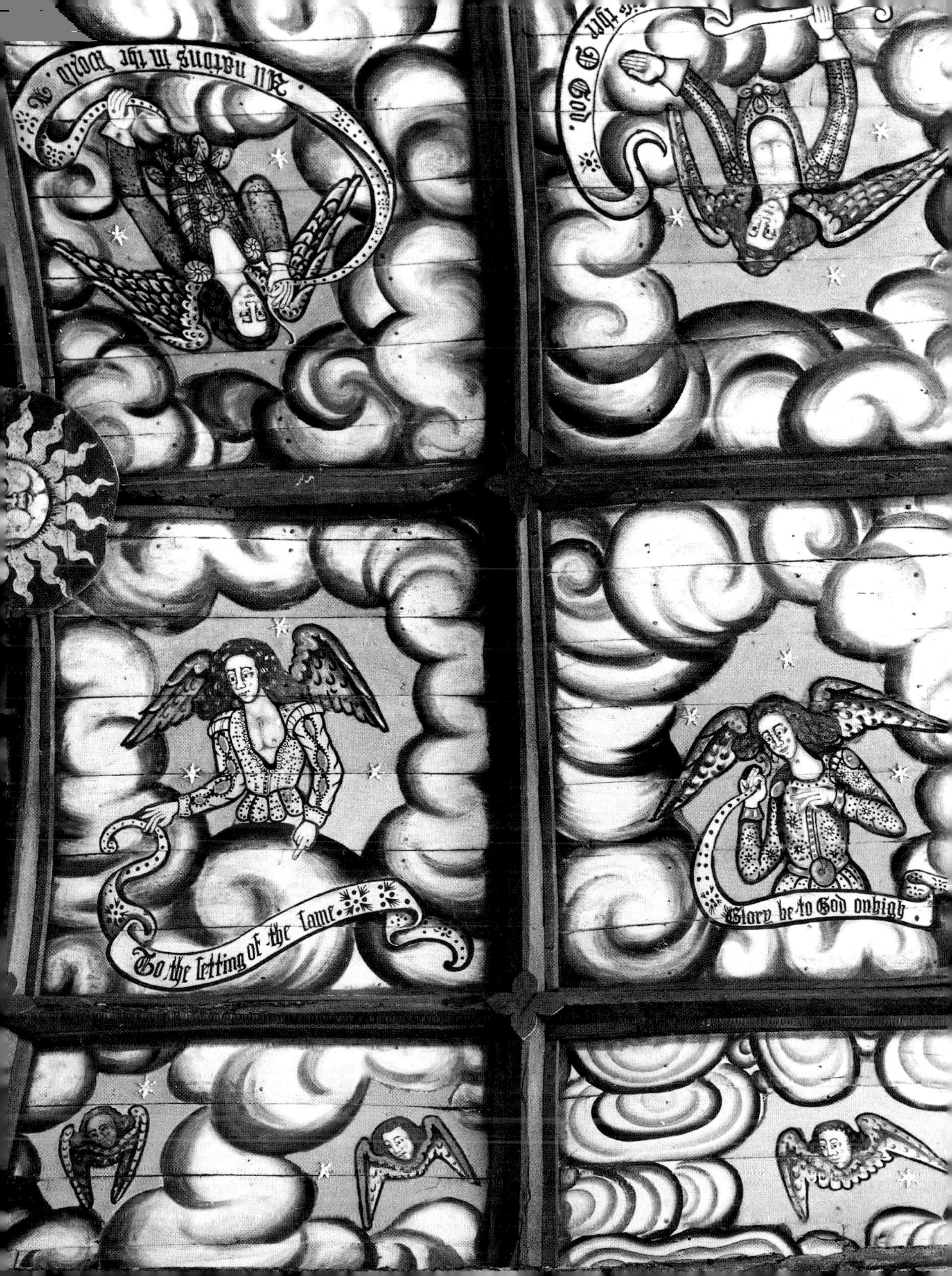
All nations in the world
that God
To the letting of the fame
Glory be to God on high

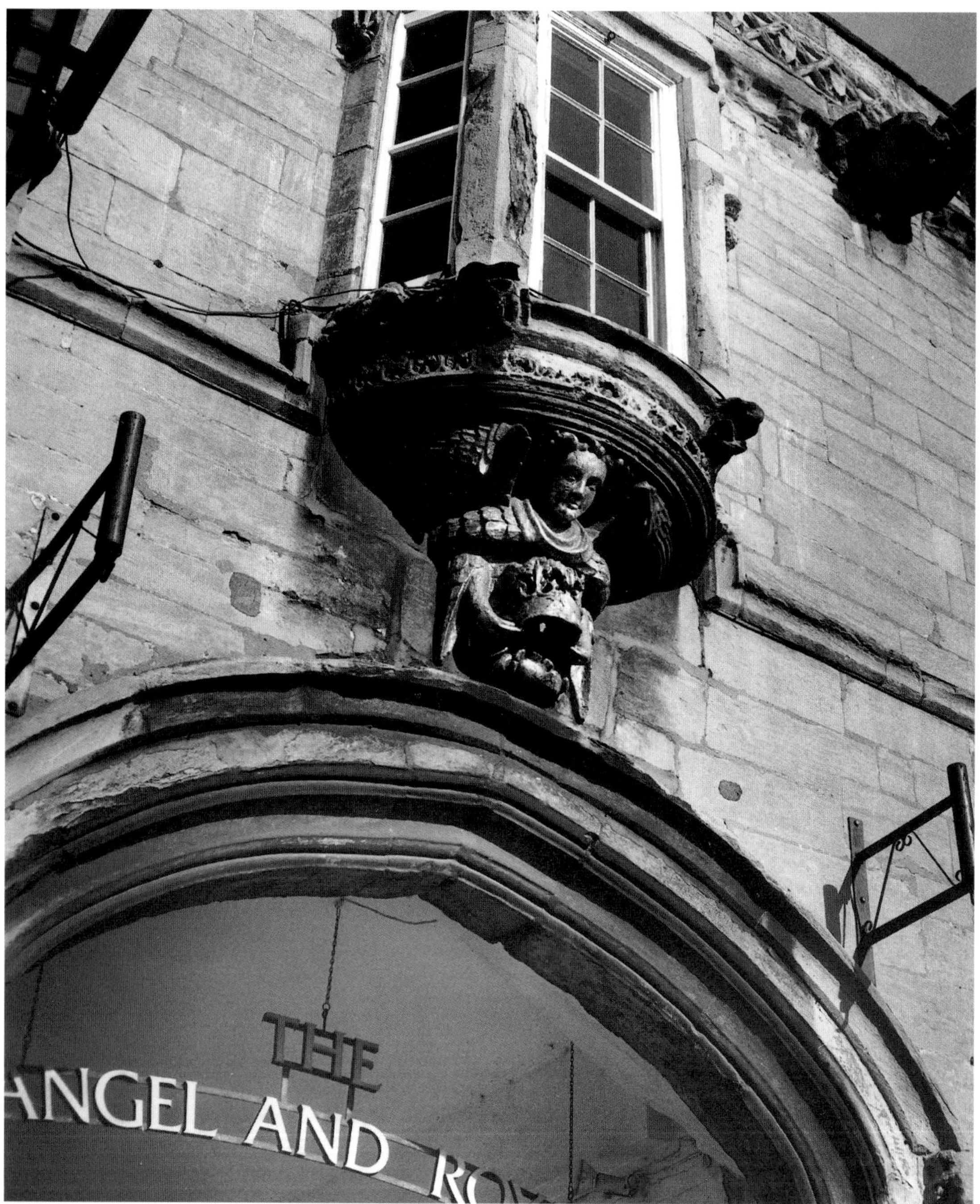

Richard III signed the death warrant of the Duke of Buckingham at this ancient coaching inn, The Angel and Royal, in Grantham. King John held court here in 1213, and Charles I visited shortly before the outbreak of the Civil War. The angel holding a crown supports an oriel window on the 15th century façade.

An angel with a coaching horn heralds the Angel Inn at Brigg. Angels first appeared on the signs of inns named the Salutation, greeting the Virgin Mary with the news that she was to give birth to the Son of God. The Virgin was removed at the Reformation, when her image was regarded as Popish idolatry, but the angels survived, and became sole keepers of some famous inns.

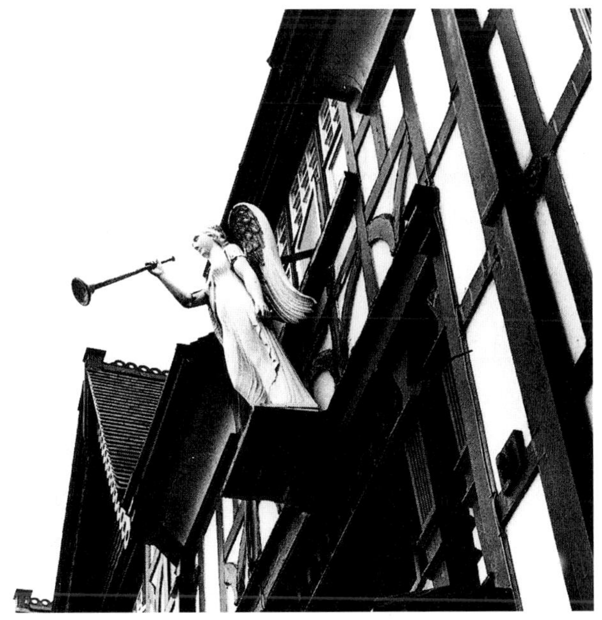

This 13th century house in Dartmouth, Devon, is now the Cherub Inn. The cherub holds a chain of stars.

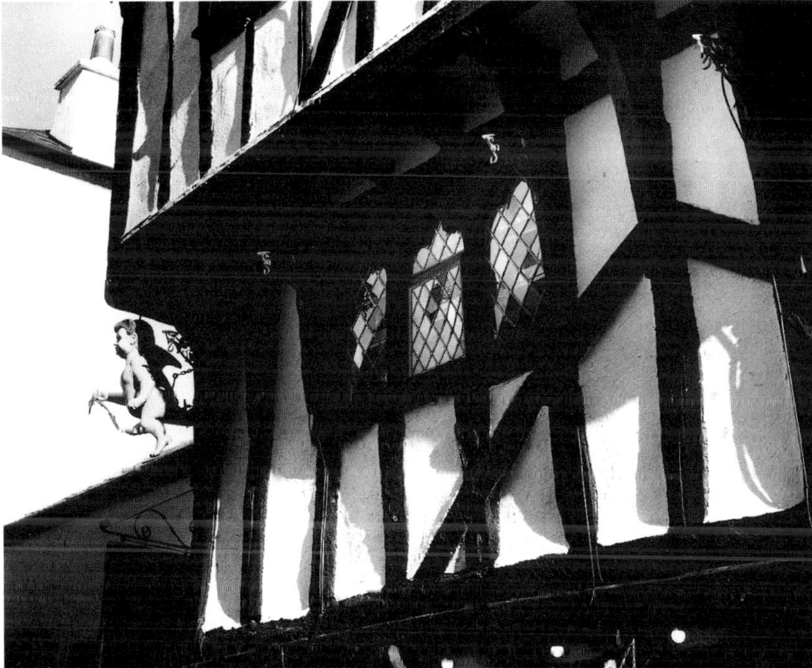

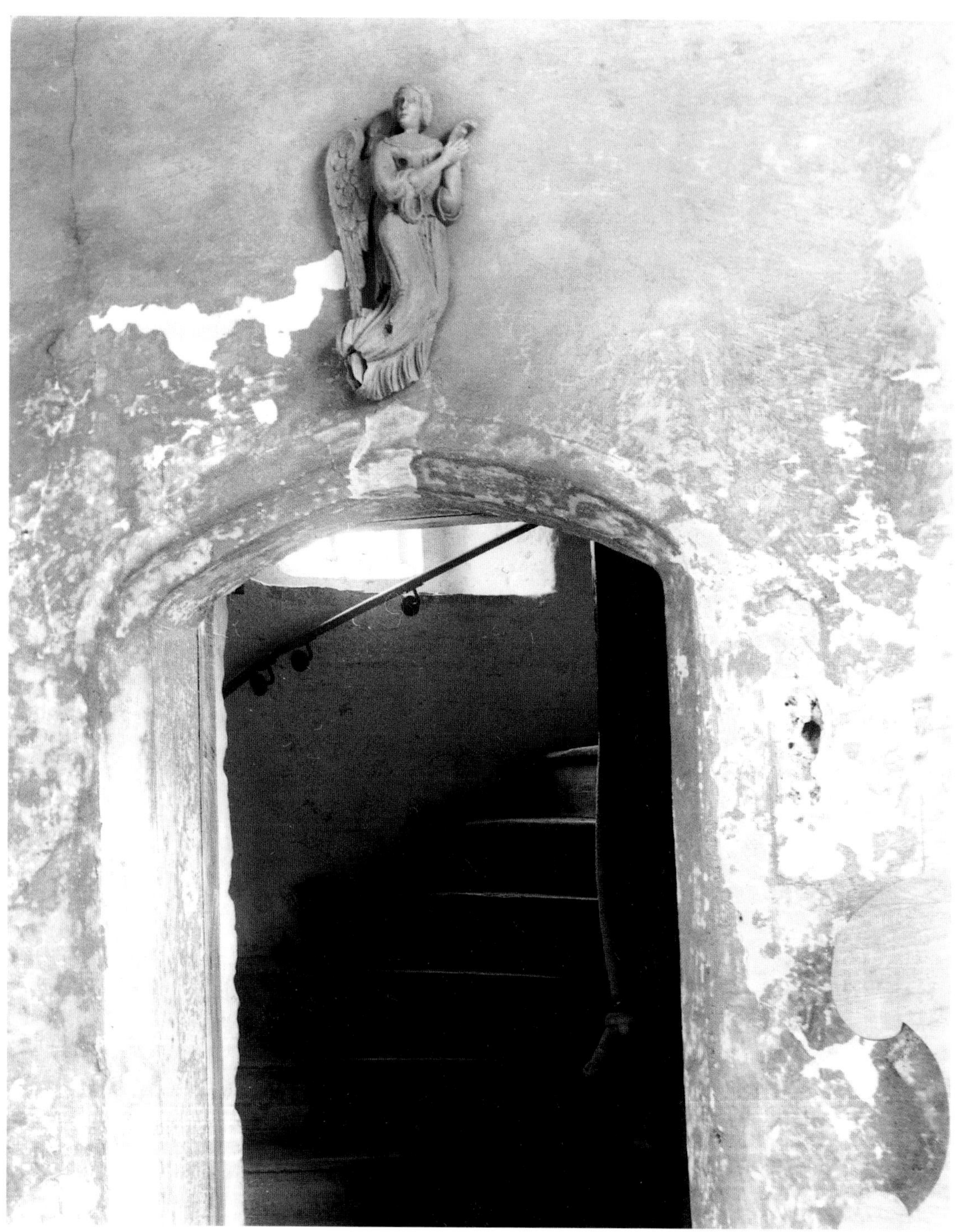

The staircase leads to Vita Sackville-West's study, in the Elizabethan Tower, Sissinghurst Castle in Kent.

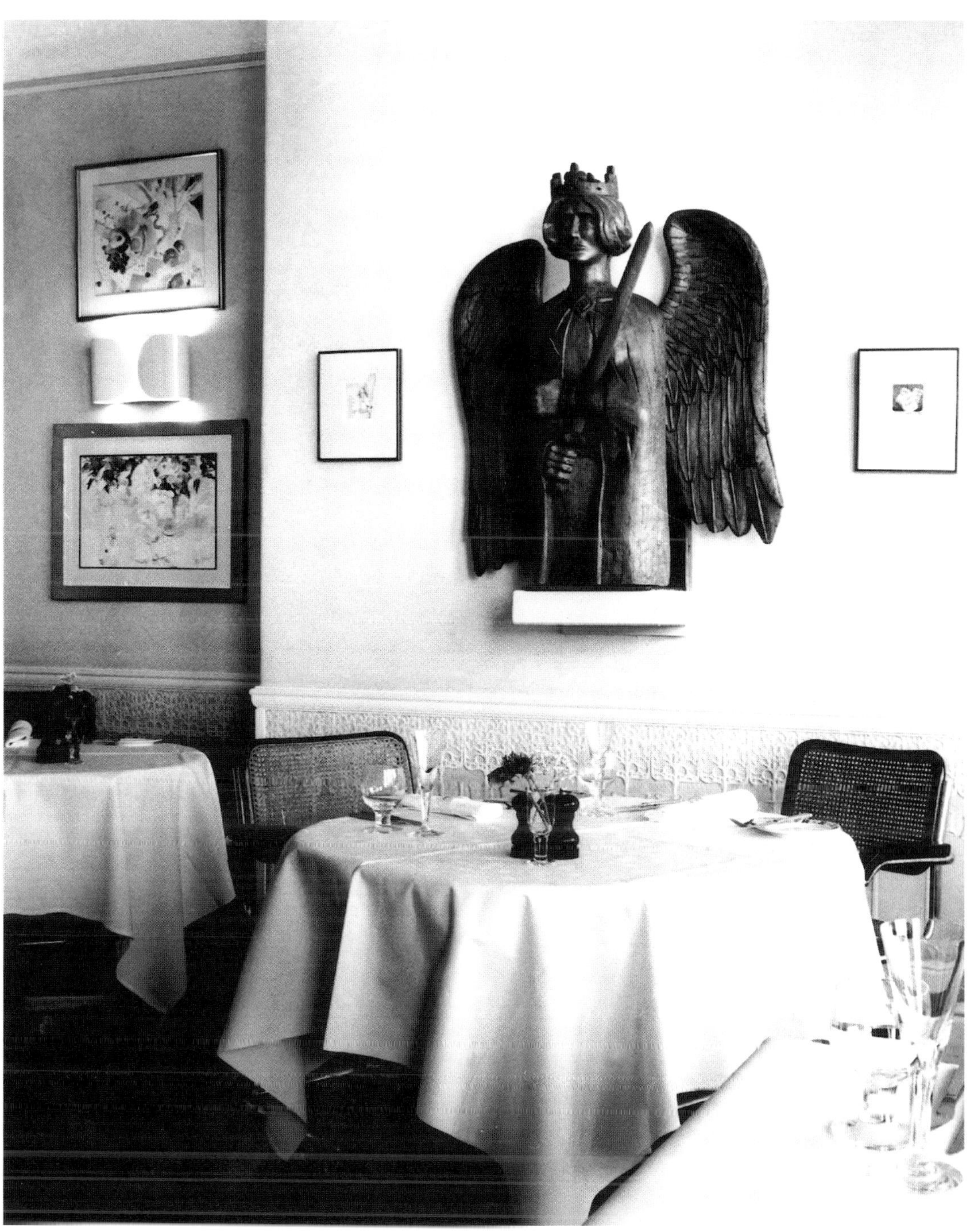

The Carved Angel Restaurant in Dartmouth, made famous by the cooking of Joyce Molyneux,
is dominated by this wooden figure, presumably St Michael, carved by a local shipwright.

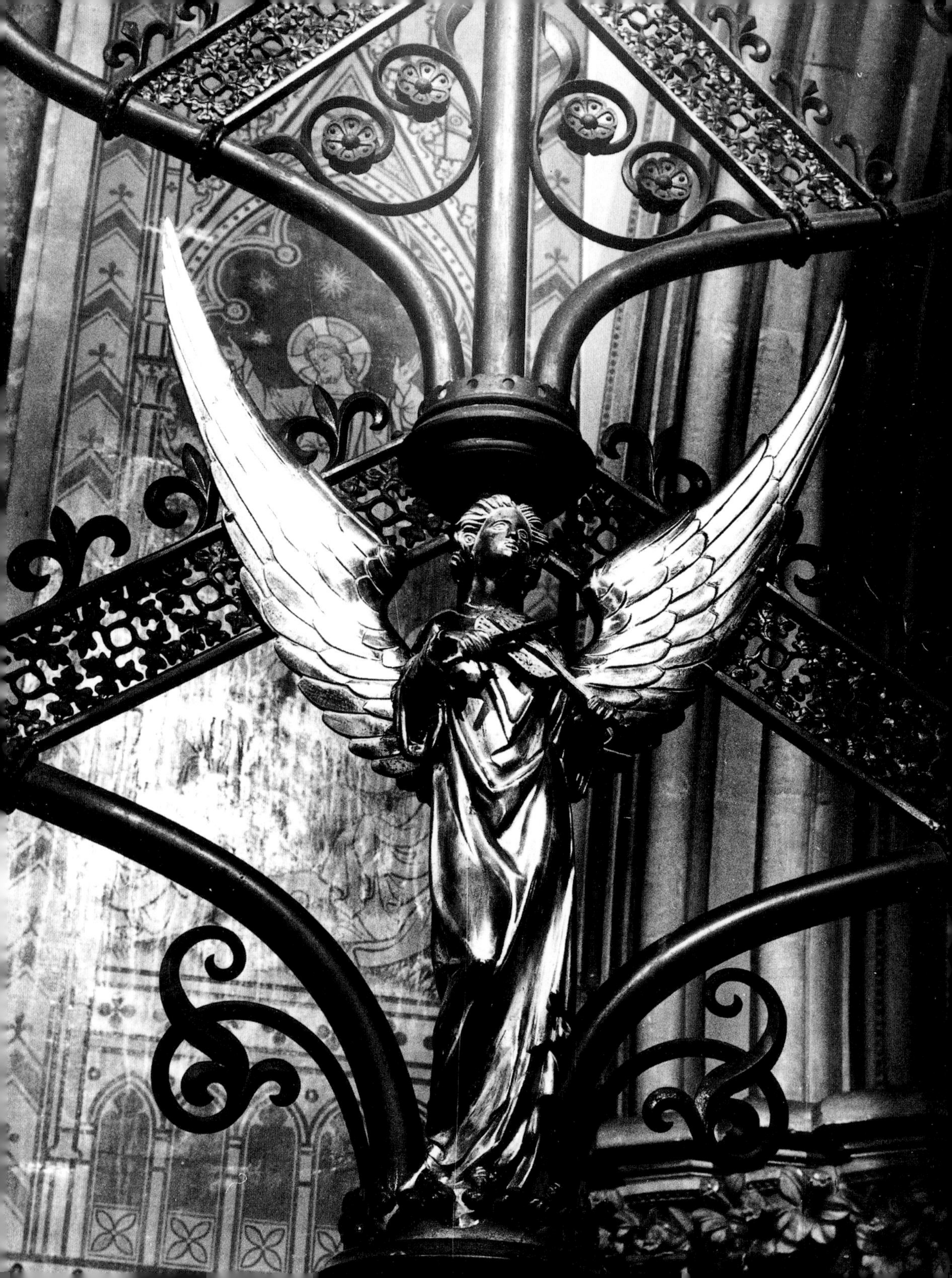

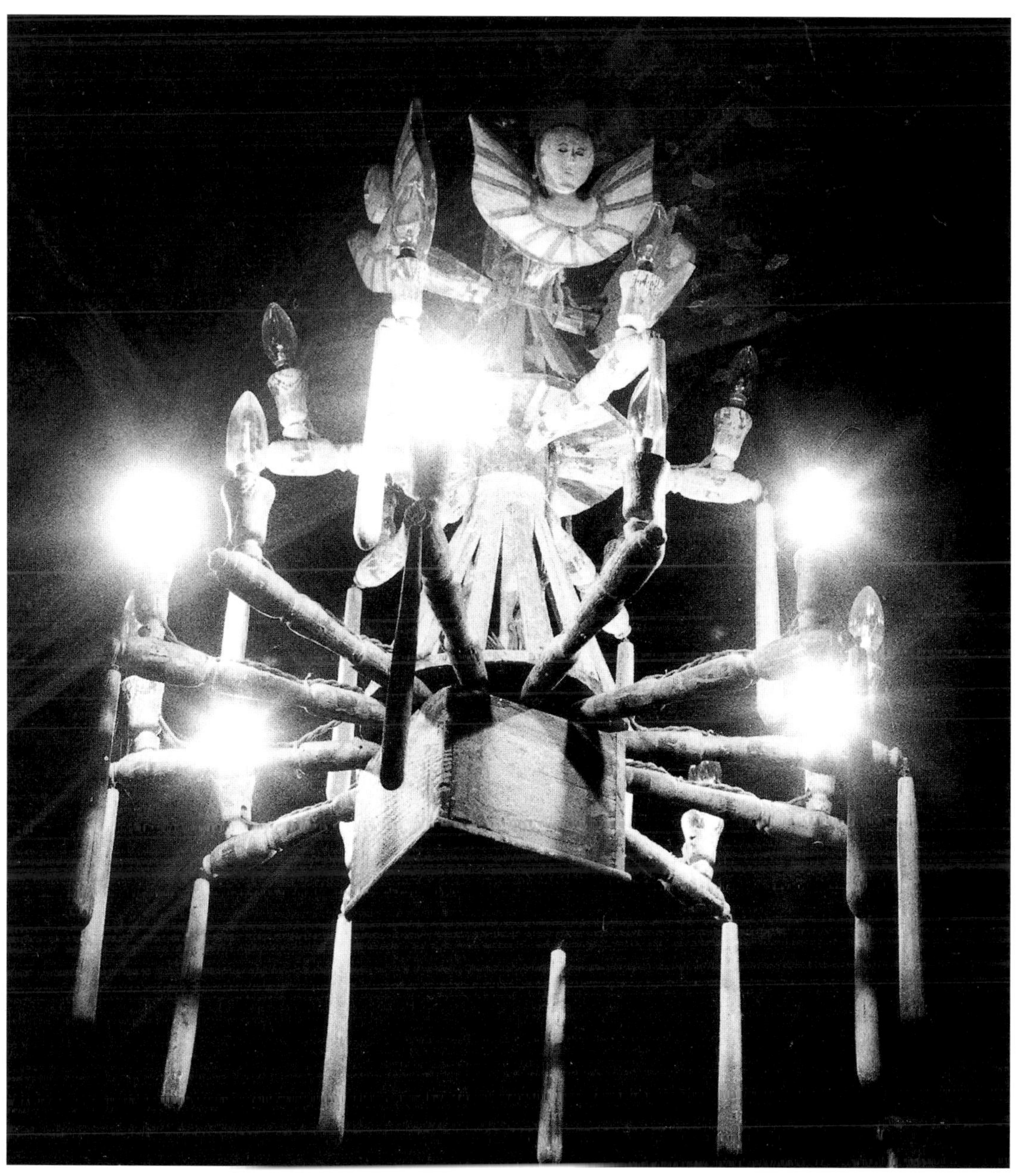

Angel chandelier in the 17th century chapel at Rhug near Corwen.

Left: The wrought iron angel candelabra at Nocton in Lincolnshire was designed by Sir George Gilbert Scott.

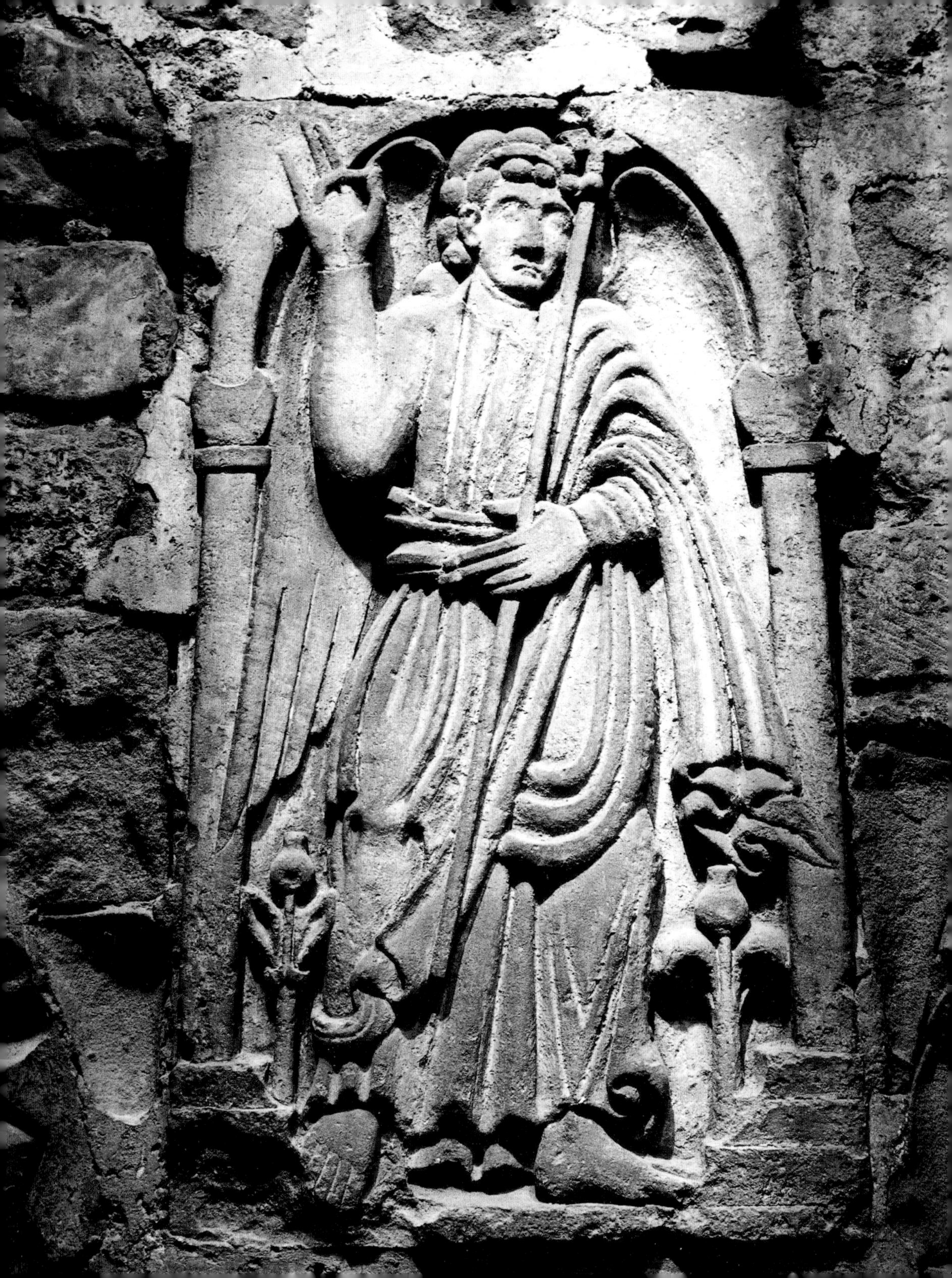

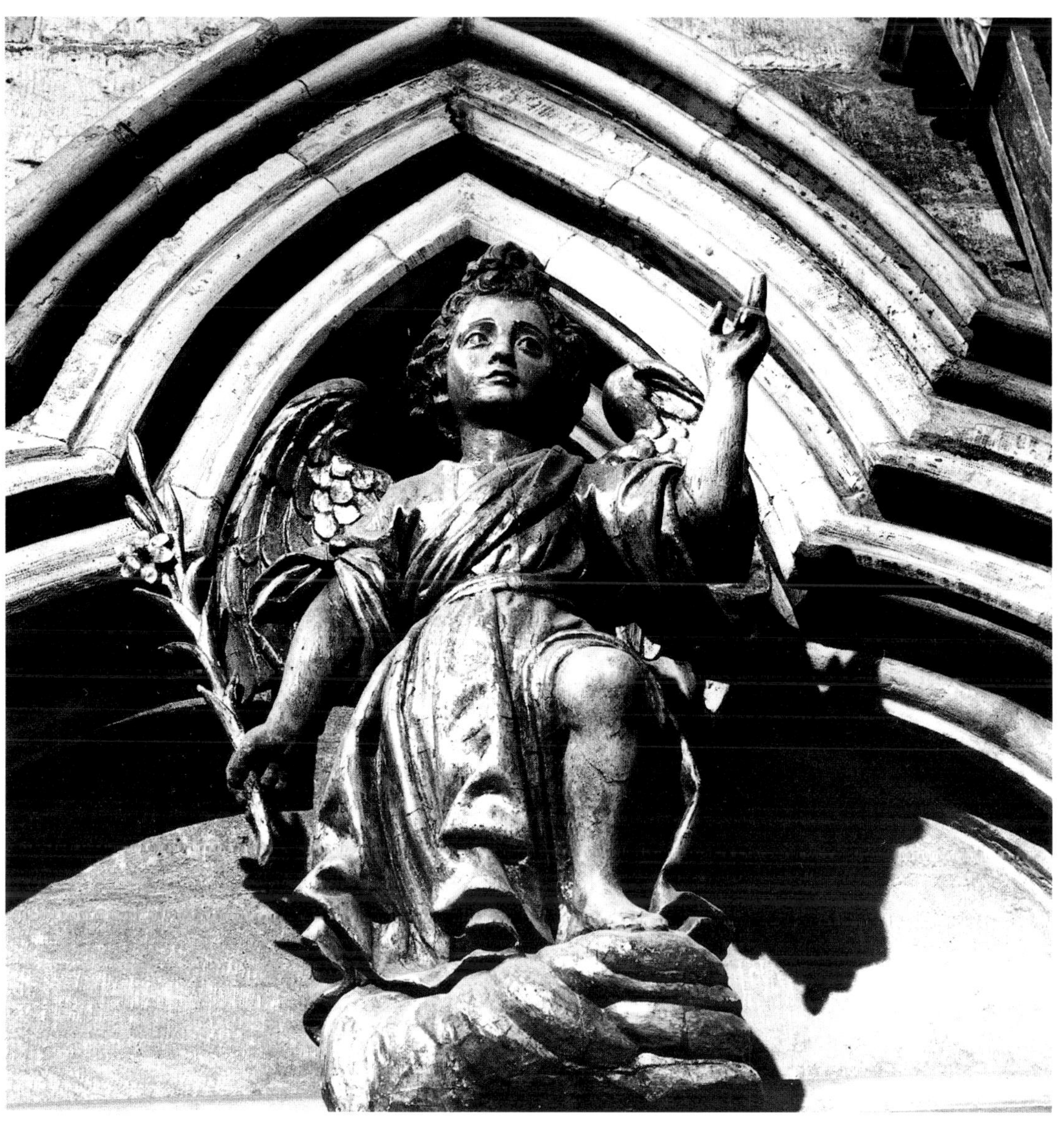

Angel of the Annunciation in York Minster.

Left: The church at Breedon-on-the-Hill in Leicestershire is full of 8th century carvings, survivors from the Saxon Priory which was destroyed by the Vikings. This 3 feet high angel is one of the finest sculptures of its period, according to Pevsner, and can be seen on request in the bell-chamber.

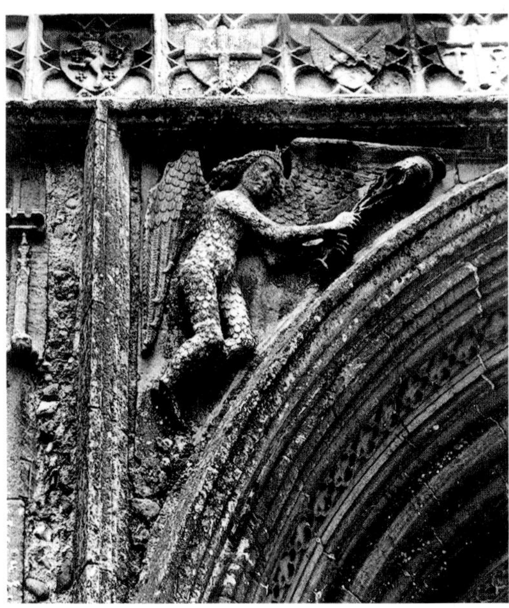

A feathered censing angel in a spandrel of the porch at Salle, Norfolk.

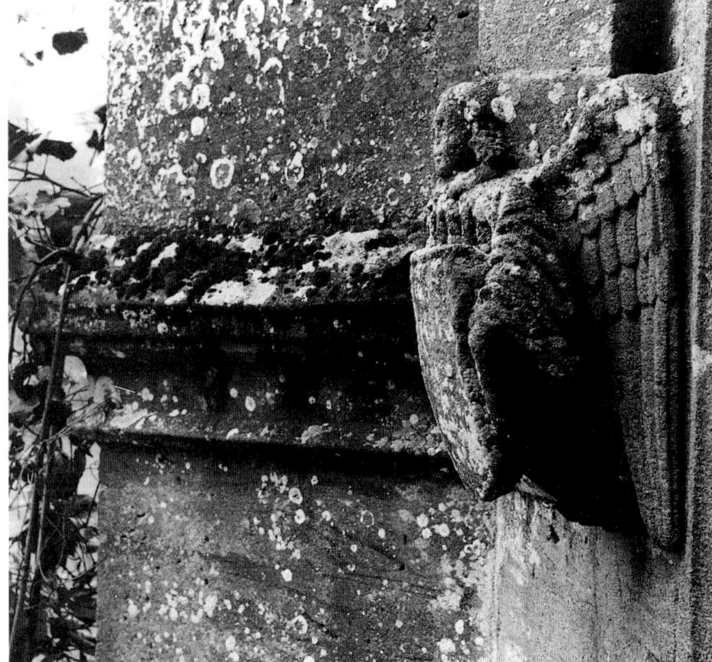

A mottled angel emerges from a wall at Forde Abbey in Dorset.

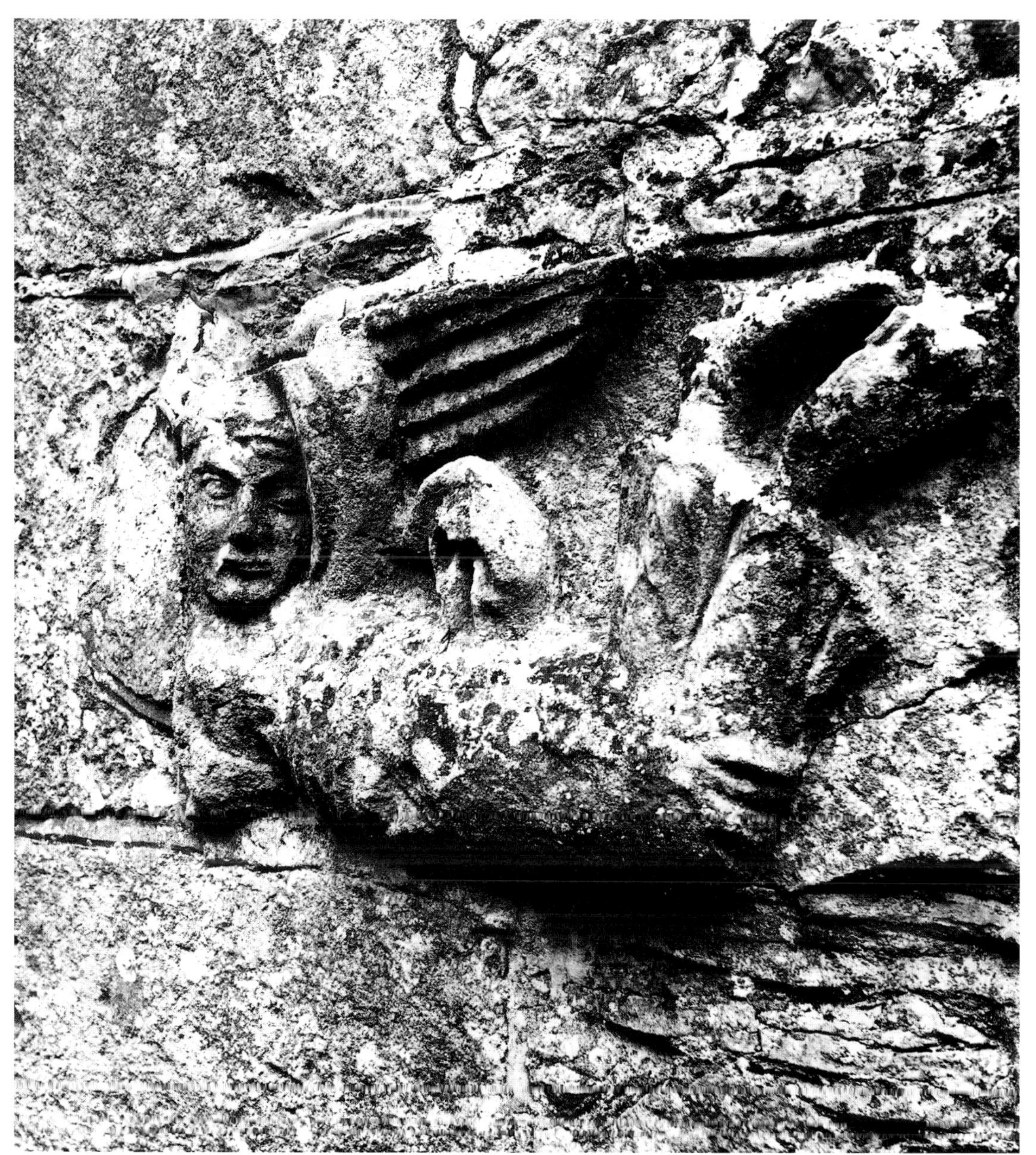

An Anglo-Saxon flying angel on the wall of the church at Winterbourne Steepleton in Dorset.

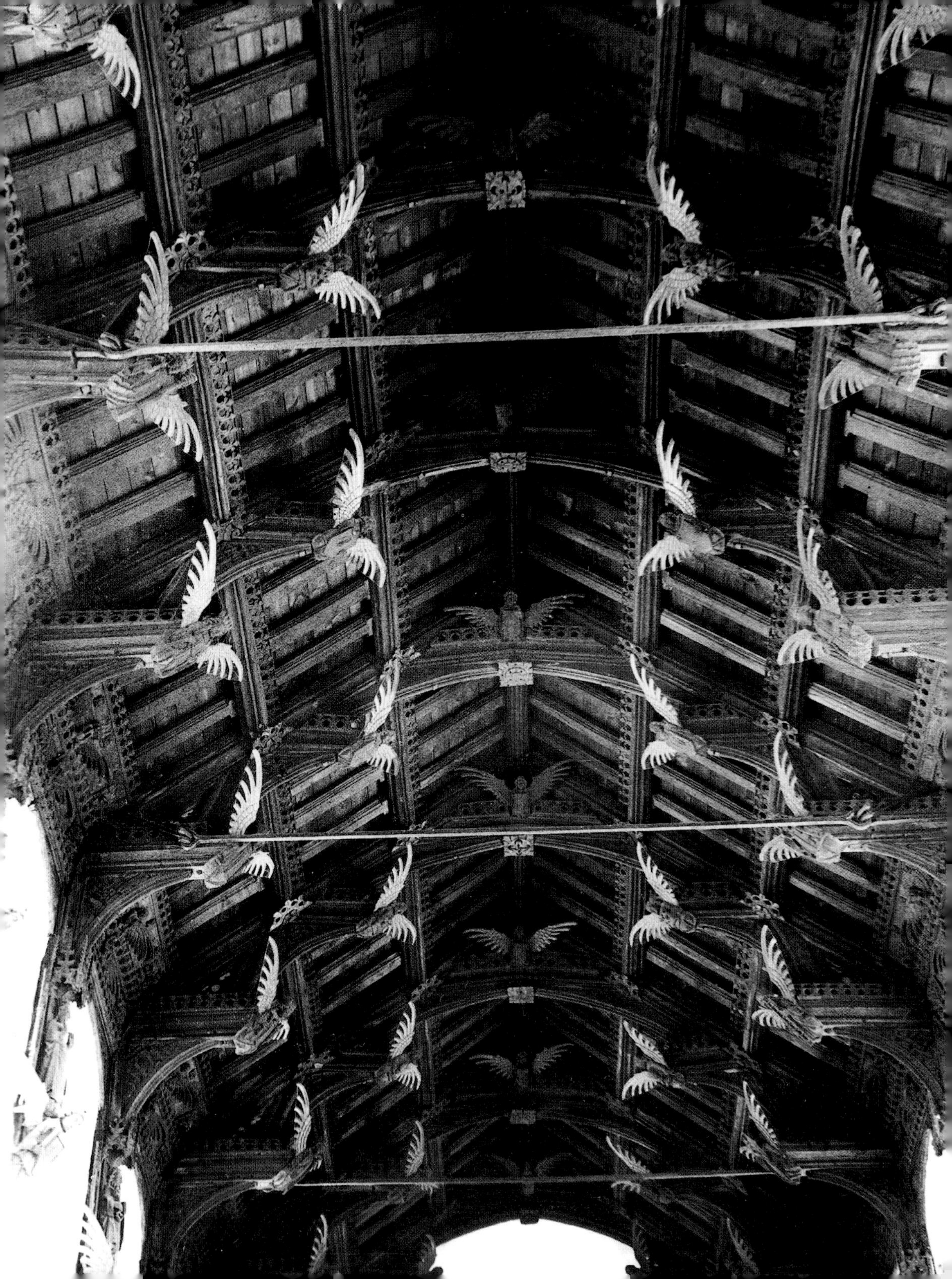

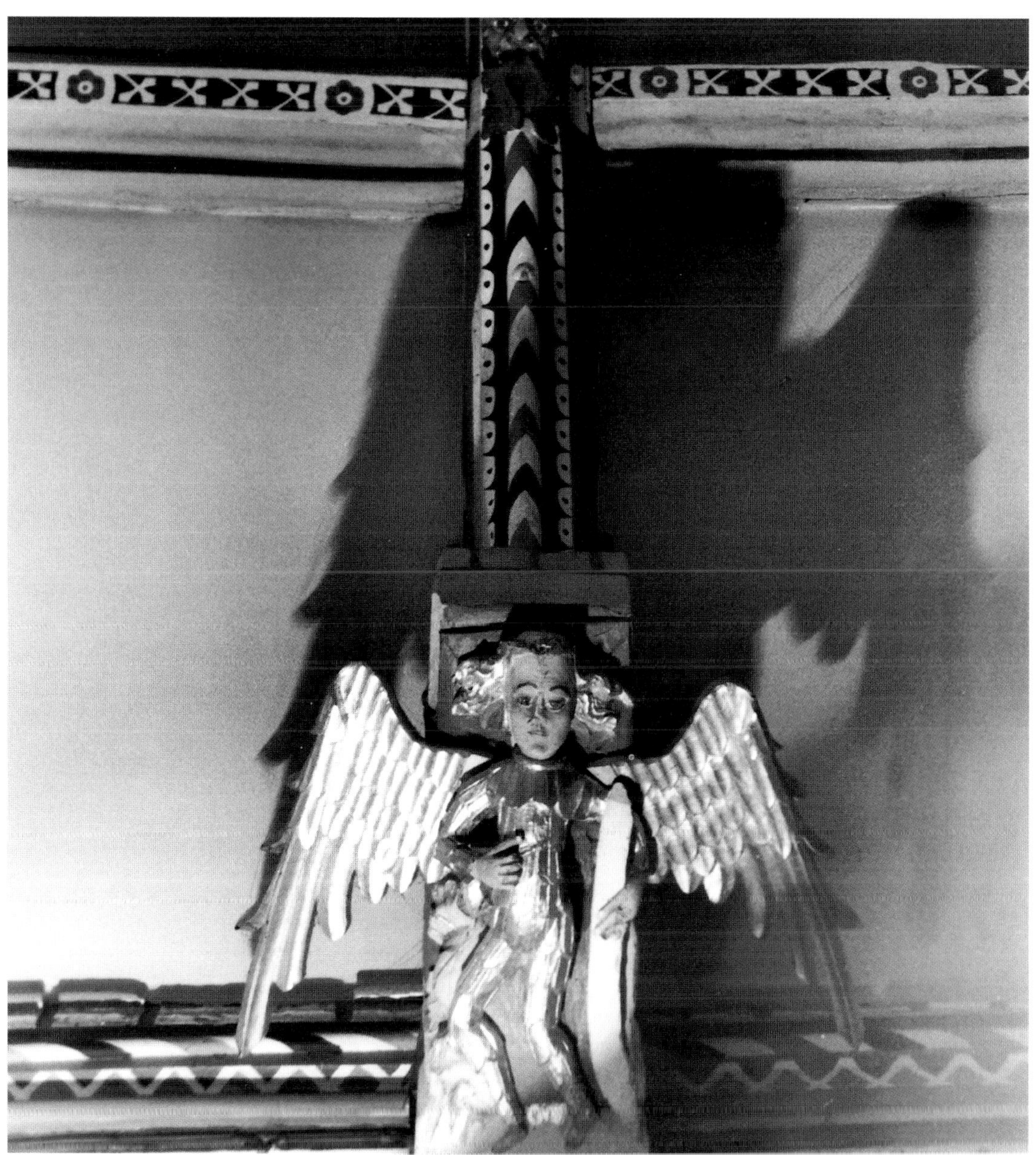

Angel bearing a scroll in North Street Church, York.

Left: March, Cambridgeshire. One of the finest of the hammerbeam angel roofs which
were such a feature of English churches in the 15th century, particularly in East Anglia.

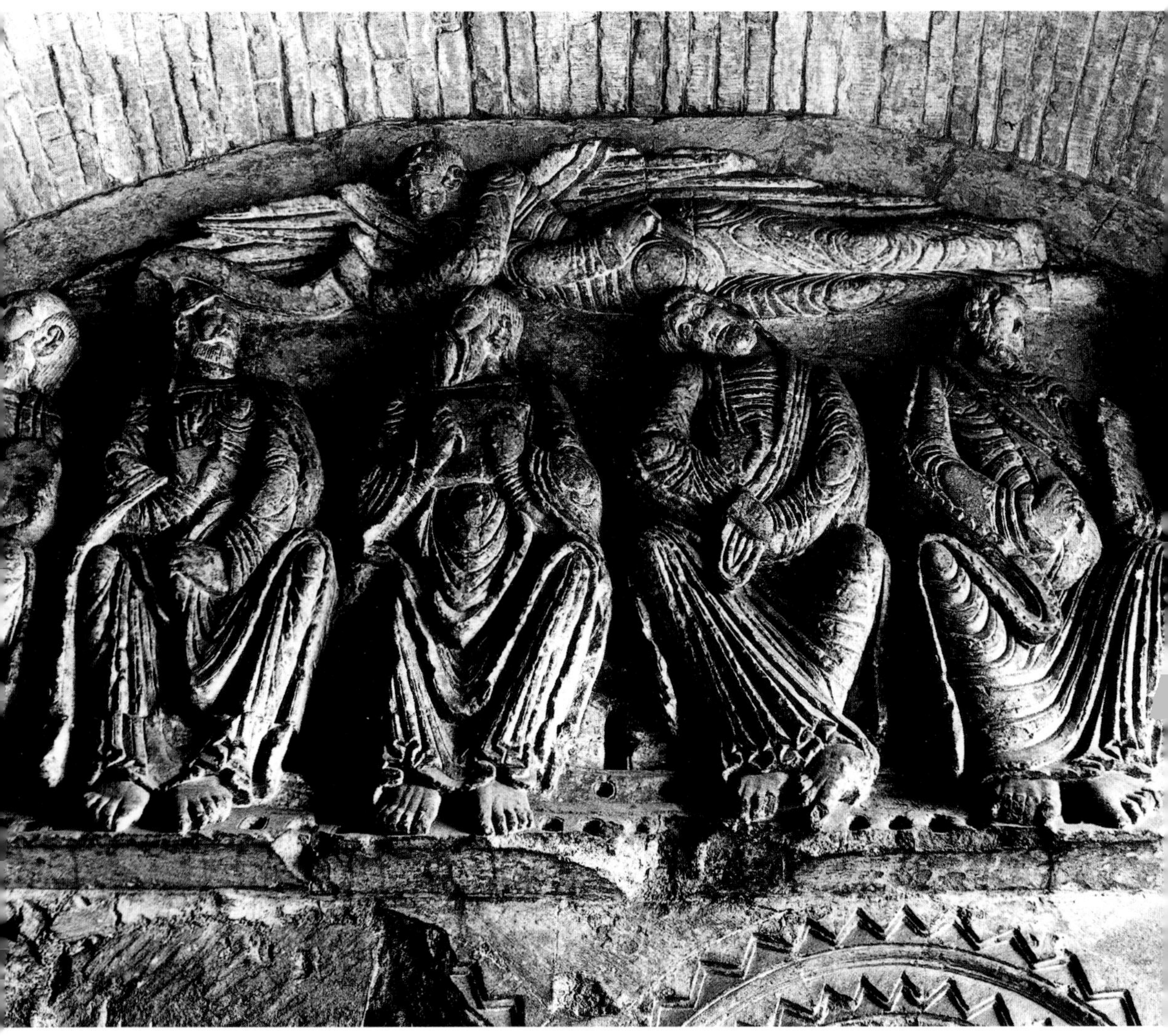

Wonderful 12th century carving in a tympanum at Malmesbury Abbey. An angel flies over the seated apostles on the day of Pentecost, bestowing upon them the gift of speaking in many languages: *And suddenly there came a sound from heaven as of a rushing mighty wind, and it filled all the house where they were sitting.*

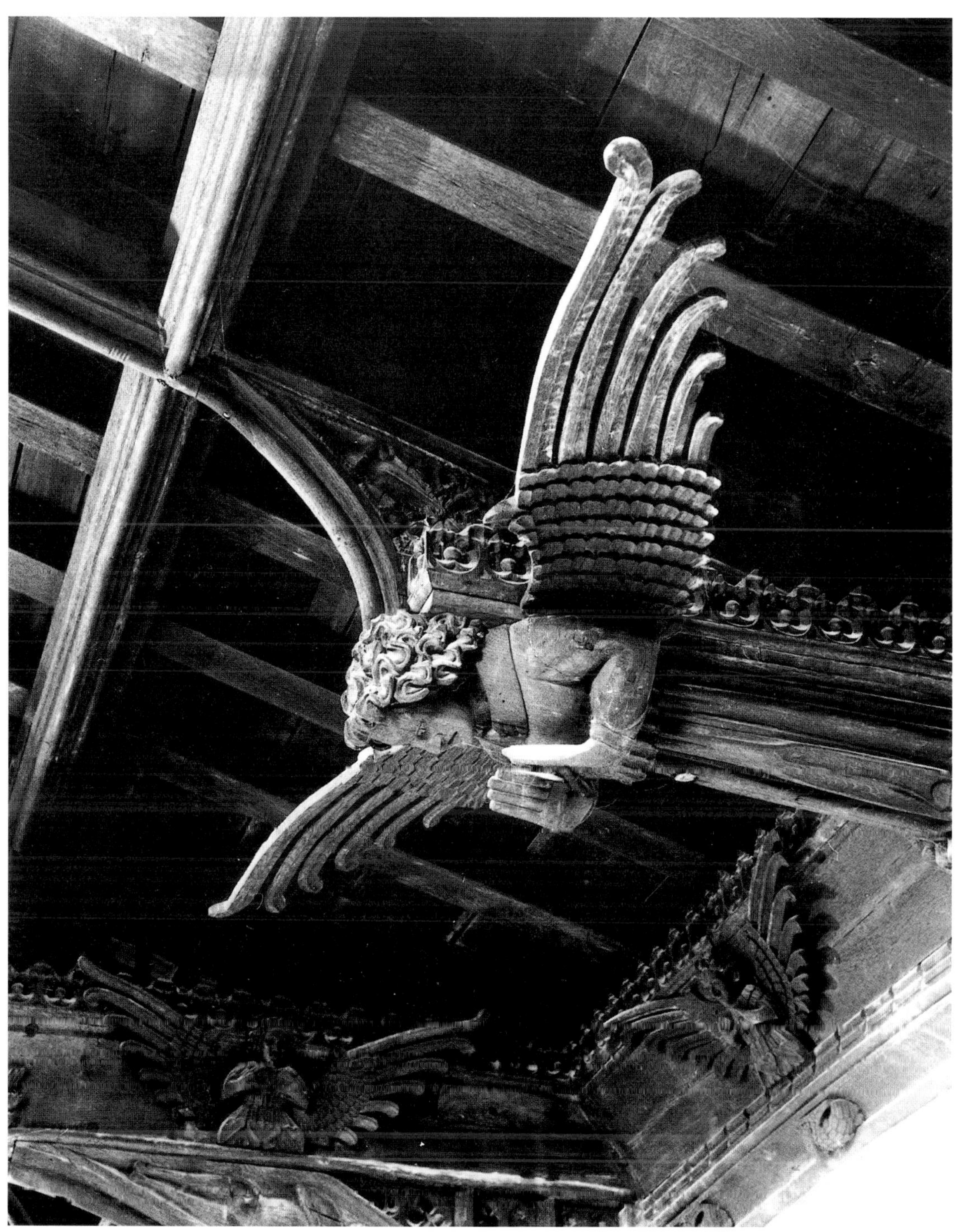

Elaborately carved angel on the roof of Upwell Church, Norfolk.

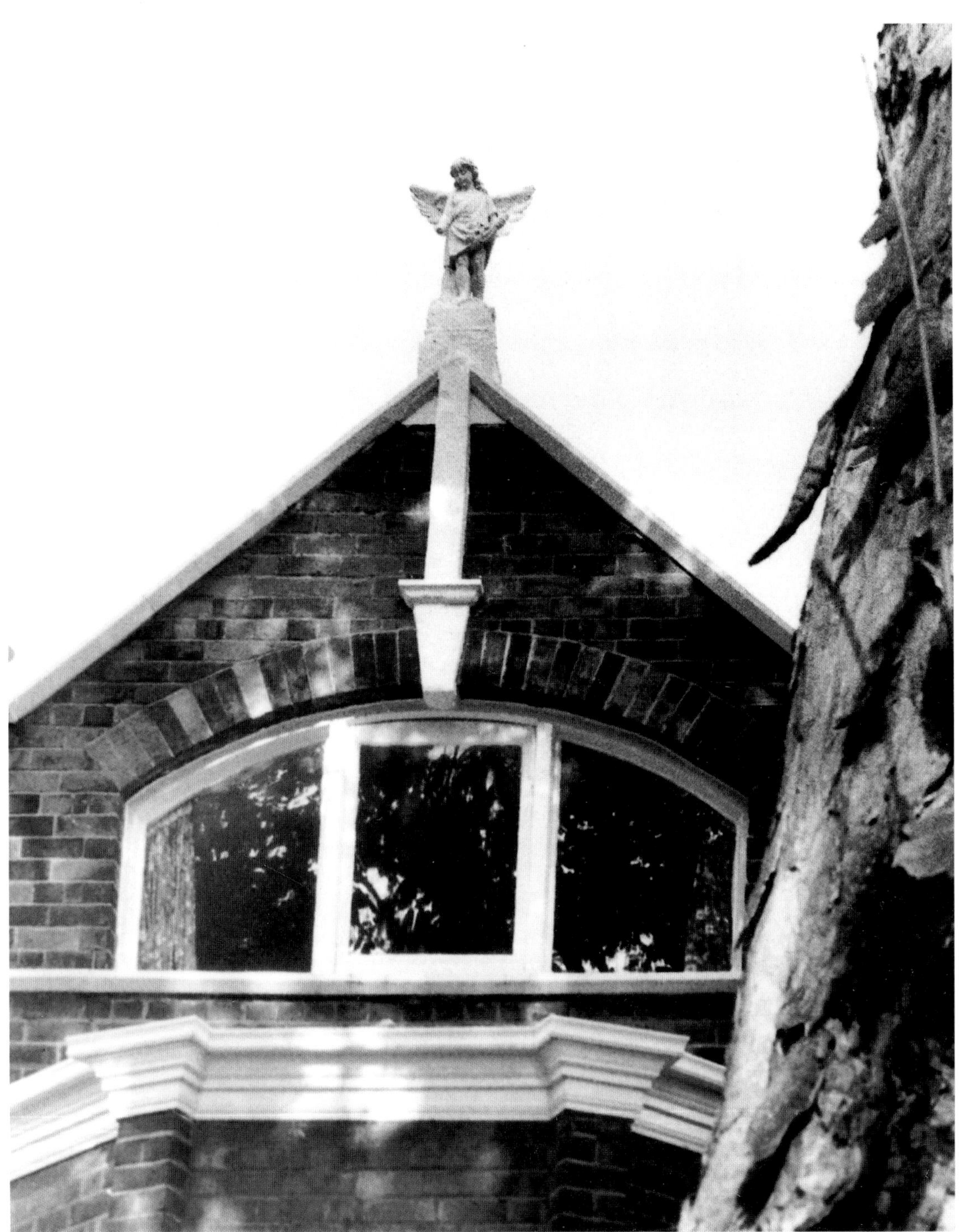

An angel guards this Victorian house in the Avenues in Hull.

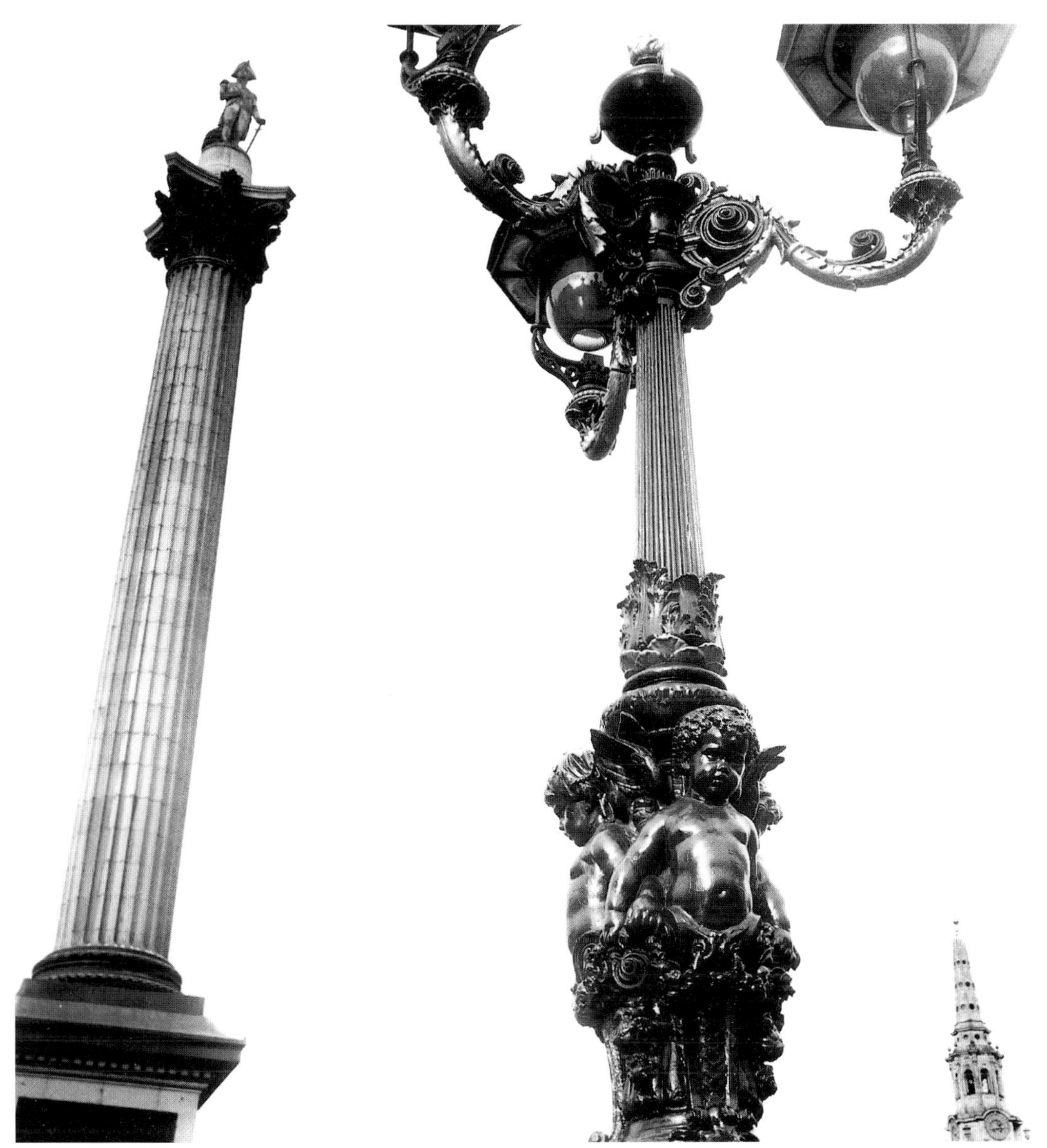

Cherubs on a lamp post in Trafalgar Square.

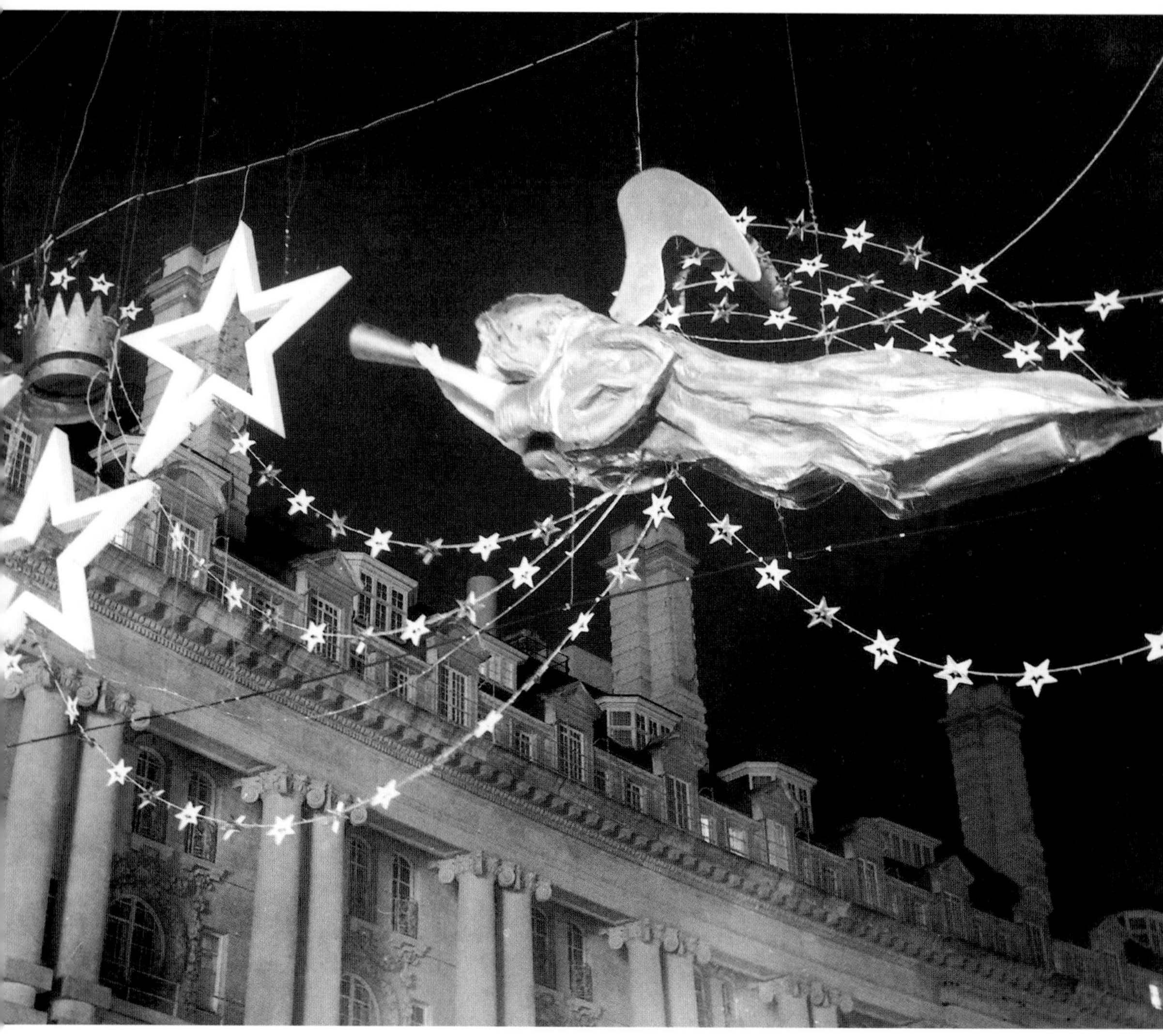

The Regent Street Christmas lights in the early 1980s, when they were switched on by the Princess of Wales.

14th century floor tile.

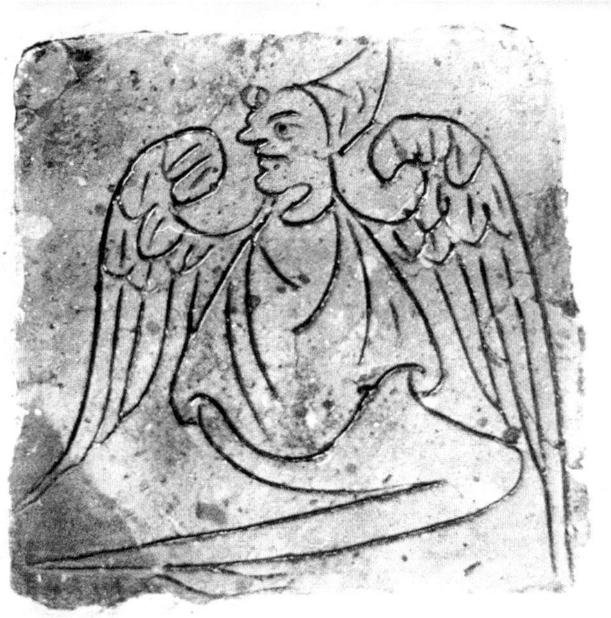

Slate engraved headstone, 1776, Michelstowe, Cornwall.

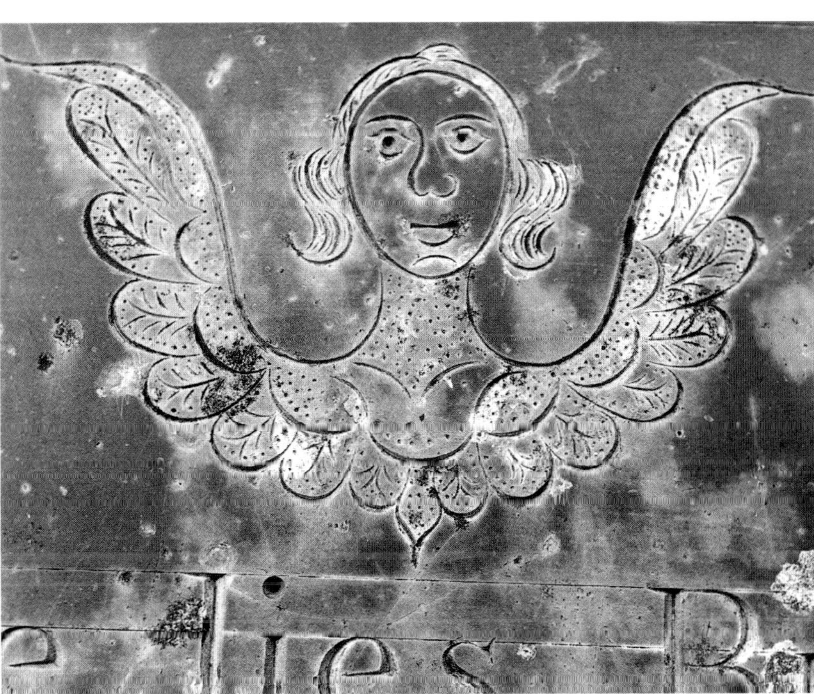

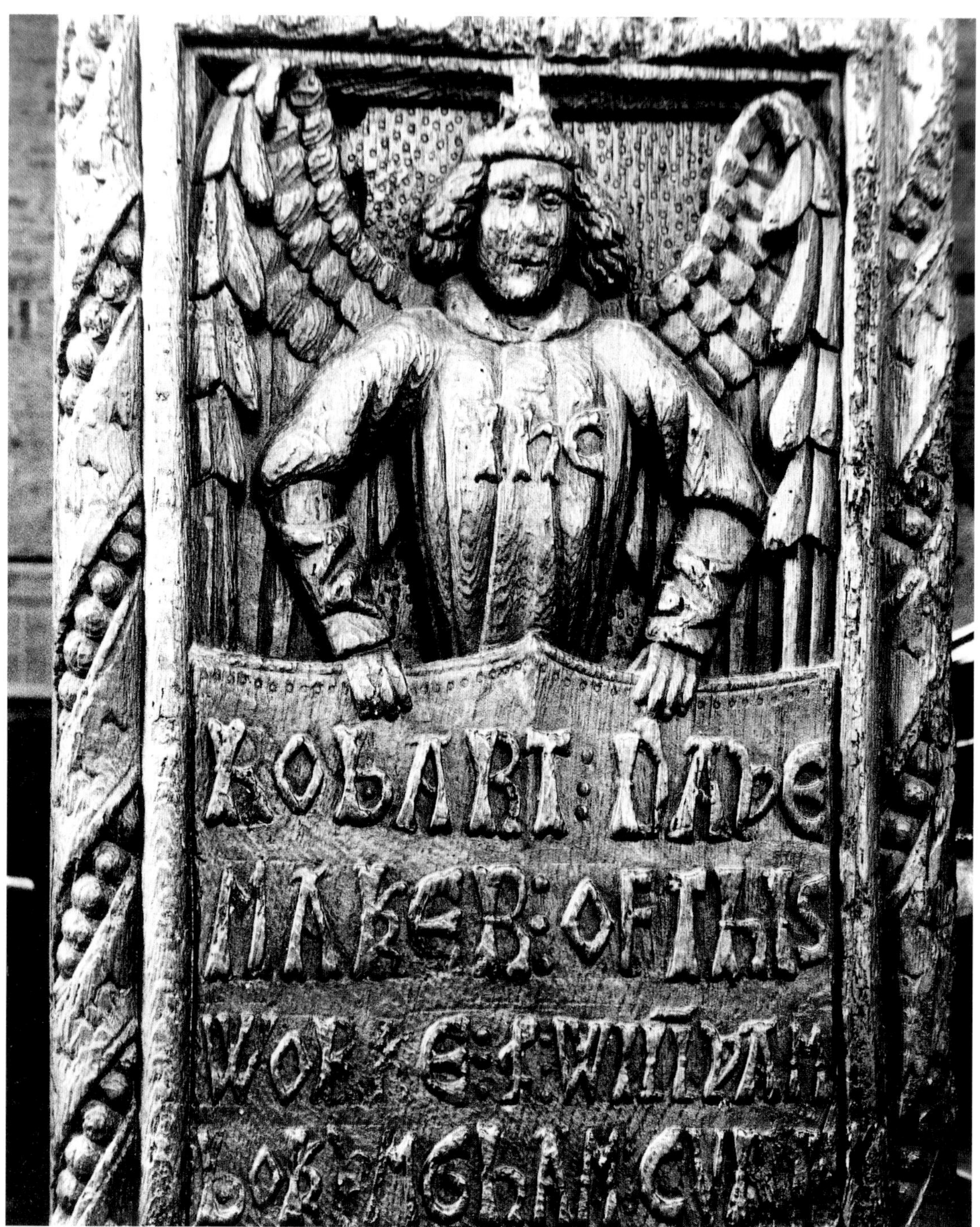

This 15th century bench end at Altarnun in Cornwall is unusual in recording the name of
its carver, Robart Daye, maker of this work, proudly displayed by an angel bearing a shield.

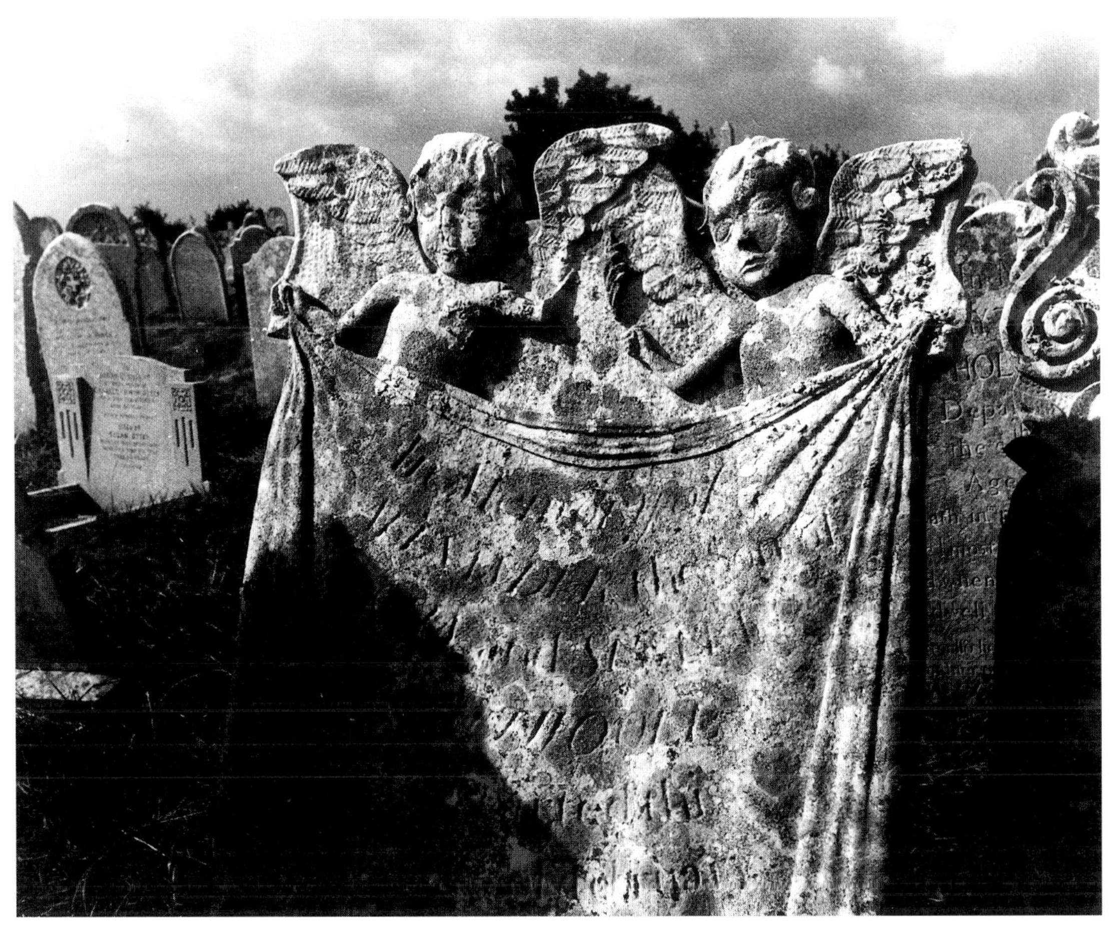

18th century headstone in the churchyard of St George's, Easton, Portland, carved from Portland ashlar, probably by the masons who were mining the stone for the church.

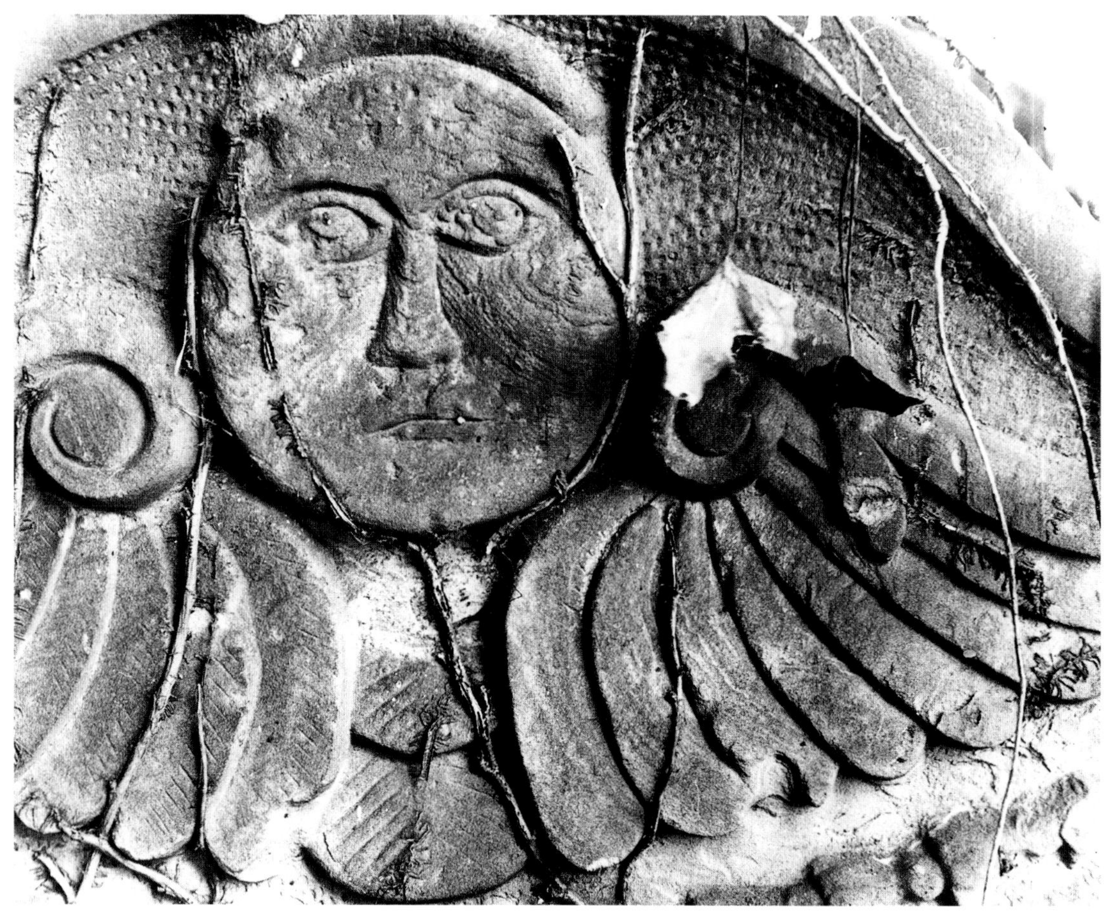

Bad-tempered angel in Skelton churchyard, North Yorkshire.

Right: An angel weeper on the
Oxenden monument in Wingham,
Kent, by Arnold Quellin.

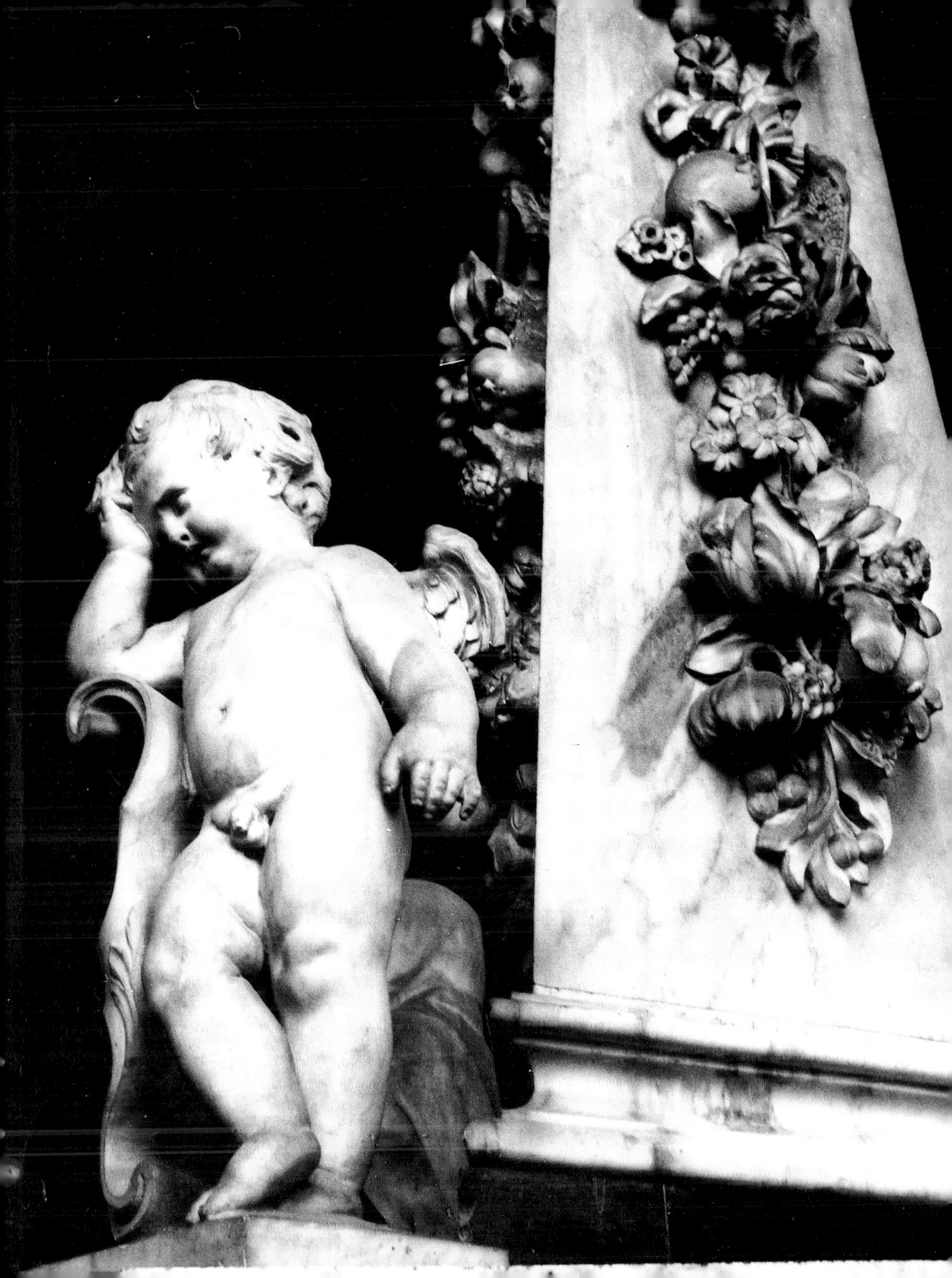

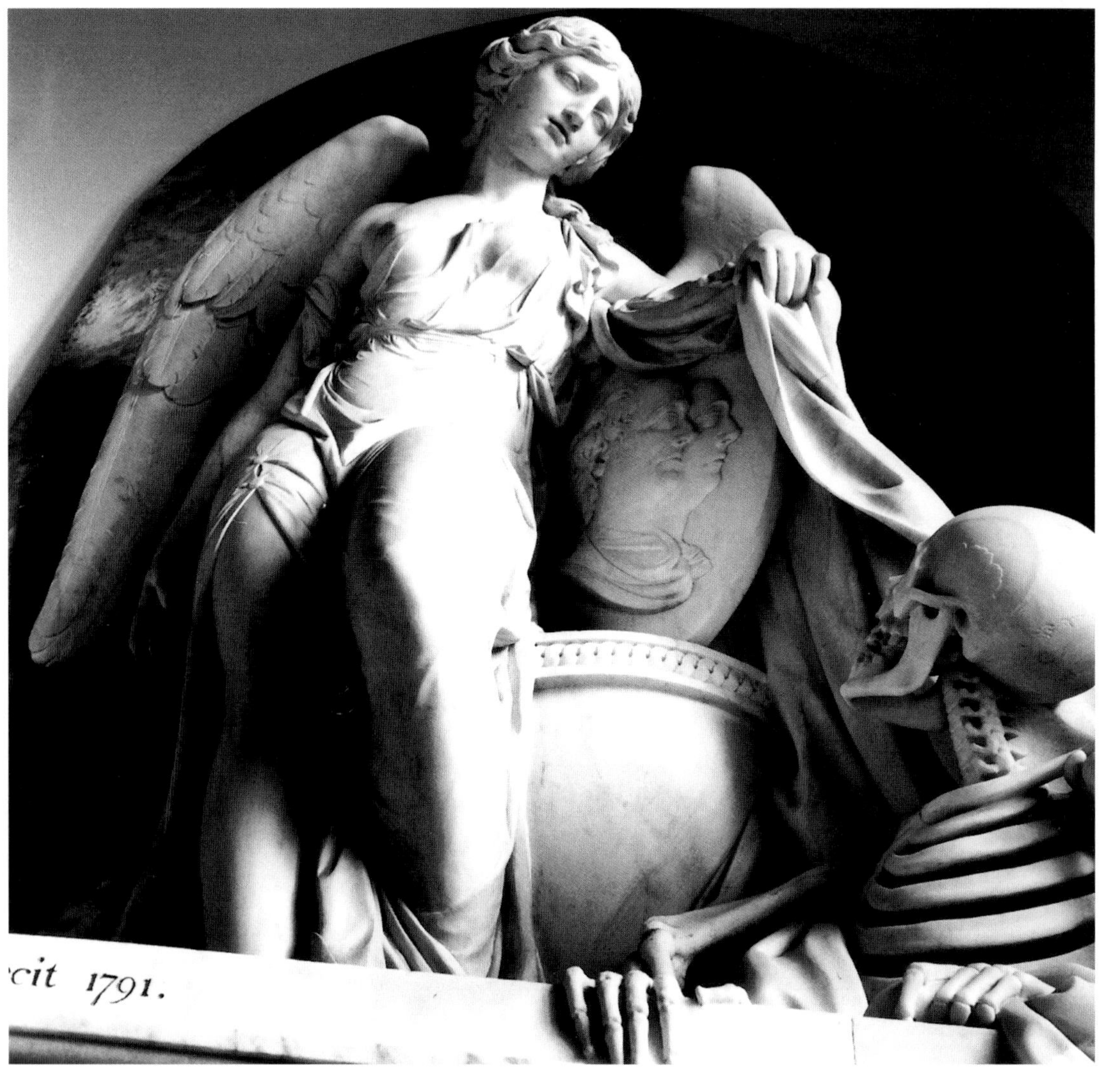

Death and the angel, on a monument by Richard Westmacott the Elder, 1791, in Sherborne church, Gloucestershire.